Henry A. Gouge

New System of Ventilation

Which has been thoroughly tested under the patronage of many distinguished

persons

Henry A. Gouge

New System of Ventilation
Which has been thoroughly tested under the patronage of many distinguished persons

ISBN/EAN: 9783337144685

Printed in Europe, USA, Canada, Australia, Japan

Cover: Foto ©Andreas Hilbeck / pixelio.de

More available books at **www.hansebooks.com**

NEW
SYSTEM OF VENTILATION

WHICH HAS BEEN

THOROUGHLY TESTED

UNDER THE PATRONAGE OF

MANY DISTINGUISHED PERSONS,

BEING ADAPTED TO

PARLORS, DINING AND SLEEPING ROOMS, KITCHENS, BASEMENTS,
CELLARS, VAULTS, WATER-CLOSETS, STABLES, PRESERVING-ROOMS,
CHURCHES, LEGISLATIVE-HALLS, SCHOOL AND COURT-ROOMS,
PRISONS, HOSPITALS, STORES, SHOW-WINDOWS, HOTELS,
BANKING-HOUSES, RESTAURANTS, COAL-MINES,
POWDER-MAGAZINES, RAILROAD TUNNELS,
FACTORIES, PORK PACKING HOUSES,
SHIPS, STEAMBOATS, ETC.
ALSO PASSENGER AND FREIGHT CARS.

A BOOK FOR THE HOUSEHOLD.

FOURTH EDITION ENLARGED, WITH NEW ILLUSTRATIONS.

By HENRY A. GOUGE.

'If we breathe a gas that is noxious, or air that contains but a very small proportion of carbonic
acid, we die."—*Anatomy, Physiology and Hygiene.* By PROF. JOHN C. DRAPER.

New York:
D. VAN NOSTRAND, 23 MURRAY AND 27 WARREN STREETS.
1881

PREFACE TO THE FOURTH EDITION.

Theories of Ventilation have had their day. Ingenious, philosophical and promising contrivances without number have been tried and found wanting, until those most impressed with the importance of Ventilation, and consequently best acquainted with the inefficiency of all methods in common use, are ready to give it up in despair, and refuse to listen to new overtures on the subject. In view of this state of things, we should consider it trifling with the public, to propound any mere *theory* of How to do it. If any positive good is to be done by this book, it must be by *plain, positive facts.* We are under the necessity of showing that ventilation is actually accomplished, for every day in the year, in spite of wind and weather; of showing how, when and where this is done; and of substantiating our assertions by an army of witnesses that cannot be resisted. This looks more like blowing our own trumpet than we could wish, in a book like this; but if there is any other practical way to treat the question, we do not know what it is. We will throw out of the book our personal experiences and testimonials, whenever any body will show us any other way to prove that such a thing as ventilation is possible.

For, what is ventilation? We suppose nobody will dispute the definition, that ventilation, in a practical sense, means the complete removal of the vitiated air and exhalations from a room *as fast as they are produced,* and the introduction of an equal supply of pure air, at the same time. Neither can it be denied that if this is what ventilation means, it presupposes *a scientific measurement of the amount* of vitiated air and exhalations produced per minute, by that number of persons, gas-lights, etc., which the room is expected to contain. Finally, having ascertained how many cubic feet of foul air must be taken out per minute, and how many of pure air brought in, there must be apparatus capable of doing just that work, and doing it regularly, under all circumstances. Nothing is worthy, therefore, to be called Ventilation, that cannot show BY MEASURE the necessary number of cubic feet of air removed every minute, the year around.

HENRY A. GOUGE.

CONTENTS.

PART I.

Ventilation: its Importance and Necessity.   Page

PART II.

What is, and What is not, Ventilation.

ILLUSTRATIONS.

IMPORTANT ADDENDUM.

While the fourth edition of this book is going through the press, late microscopic discoveries come to hand which double the proof of our theory that the diseases of civilization result mainly from the detention or obstruction of air by the walls of civilized habitations. The *Medical Record* of June 18, 1881, contains an elaborate review by Prof. James Law, of the more advanced microscopic researches and experiments on the organic germs of disease. It is settled that these poisonous germs, or bacteria, are identical in all respects, microscopically, with others that are perfectly harmless; and that the simple rule for rendering either class harmless or destructive is to give them more or less oxygen. For instance, the germ of the terrible malignant pustule itself is rendered harmless by free oxygenation, while its innocent *fac simile*, developed in an infusion of hay, if afforded a limited supply of oxygen, becomes as deadly as the other and produces the same disease by inoculation. The explanation is simple : that bacteria developed with copious oxygen cannot live without it, and hence fail to propagate or survive within the bloodvessels.

A beautiful harmony is here conspicuous in the purposes of Nature, which it behooves us to fall in with. It seems that that stage in the cycle of life and death which has hitherto exhaled infectious germs for the untimely destruction of the living, was not meant to do this, but has been perverted to an abnormal result by the same mistake which all house-dwellers make in checking the circulation and supply of oxygen. All that is needed to heal the very fountain of disease, is to supply its products with oxygen, for a healthy development according to the intention of Nature.

We have here a new reason for the remarkable preservation of organic matter as well as human health in certain exceptionally pure atmospheres. It is nothing but copious oxygen. Pure air, if supplied in constant profusion, is the great antiseptic or disinfectant, and nothing can supply any part of its place for a moment, not even the extremest cold. The putrefaction of walrus meat at fifty degrees below zero, which so astonished Dr. Kane in the arctic regions, has been often matched in the experience of packers in this country, when meat has been suddenly frozen on the surface, sealing up the internal germs from the air. [See Dr. Kane's experience, page 27.]

These truths are not altogether new, but the latest science has put them in a new light and a new shape, so that he who runs may read.

Man was not made to die of disease, but has brought it upon himself, through ignorance of the necessity and means of thoroughly ventilating his dwellings.

VENTILATION.

PART I.

The more we reflect on the facts or the philosophy of life in enclosed air, as compared with life in the free and open atmosphere, the more we are inclined to think that the strongest advocates of ventilation have hardly begun to appreciate its importance. It is an undisputed fact, that air and exhalations more or less confined are invariable antecedents of the majority of diseases. On the other hand, free air is the *sine qua non* among all the conditions under which Nature is enabled to repel disease on a general scale. What can be more evident than that the diseases of civilization, universally and almost solely bred and harbored within domestic walls, must have their origin in the fermentation of confined organic matter, since the detention of such matter is the single necessary result of inhabited enclosures.

Add to the blood-poison of organic decay the nerve-poison of the deadly narcotic, carbonic acid, and we have stated, substantially, the sources of disease and death that are peculiar to house-protected existence, and that must account for its almost pestilent sickliness in comparison with life in the open air, notwithstanding favorable differences in almost every other respect.

To illustrate the effect of but partial detention of organic exhalations, we have only to refer to the miasmata of low lands, detained, not by perpendicular and enclosing walls, but by mere rising ground and dense vegetation from being freely dispersed by the winds; thus creating lairs for pestilence of every grade, from ague to yellow fever and Asiatic cholera. Is it incredible, that a box like a house, completely enclosing a number of persons, should detain their exhalations to a sufficient extent to account for much vital degeneracy in the long run, with many characteristic diseases, even though windows, doors and chimneys were kept as freely open as possible? Such are, undeniably, the coincidences of fact.

It is true that there is an improvement manifest in vital statistics, and in every one's observation of the general health and longevity. Possibly it may be asked, How is it that former generations have not done better than the present, instead of doing worse, since their more primitive habitations admitted air so much more freely than ours? This question is fruitful of suggestive considerations. A large number of what might be called violent deaths, especially in infancy and age, formerly resulted from exposures, from bad diet, from want of care or medical knowledge, and from other causes now vastly ameliorated. But in constitutional vigor, and in freedom from complicated and chronic diseases, the advantage remains undoubtedly with our predecessors. It is true, that children and old people do not perish from exposure and neglect to any such extent as formerly. But whether the number of those who reach old age is fully sustained, (apart from the increased number who reach maturity) is another question. At all events, there seems to be no improvement, but rather the reverse, in respect to the chronic and proverbial inferiority of life in houses to life out of doors. It cannot be doubted—at least, so far as we know, it is not doubted—that free and therefore fresh air, is the great secret of health, with those who live in it. Why should we doubt, then, the converse proposition, which is only the same thing in other words, that confined or obstructed air is the great source of sickness and infirmity?

If these things are so, ventilation takes almost the first place among the interests of humanity and of every individual. At the same time, and by the same argument, it is a subject yet to be understood, and an object yet to be realized on the general scale. Nevertheless, it is a fact, to be hereinafter demonstrated, that the breath of life within doors can be made as pure and healthful as the open air

ZYMOTIC DISEASES—FOUL AIR—NATIONAL HOTEL DISEASE—
HOSPITAL VENTILATION.

We hope that the new medical phrase, "zymotic
diseases," will neither puzzle nor frighten our readers, the
greater proportion of whom are probably not physicians.
Translated into plain English, it means simply "*diseases
from foul air*," and the subject should be better understood
than it seems to be, both theoretically and practically. It
is intimately connected with the subject of ventilation, and
as such we give it a prominent place in our book. When
intelligent people understand that a large proportion of the
deaths occurring in our midst are the result of foul air, they
will be more cautious than they are about breathing it, and
will be more disposed than at present to have their houses
and places of business ventilated.

When physicians tell us that certain diseases are produced by foul air, we understand it to be the result of
atmospheric poison, in some form or other, which is capable, when taken into the system by the breathing process,
of generating disease, just as disease is generated by taking
a drug-poison into the system by the mouth. The practical
inference from these statements is obvious. If an individual
does not wish to suffer from a drug-poison, as for example
prussic acid, he will be careful not to swallow prussic acid.
If he does not wish to suffer from a zymotic disease, he will
be equally careful not to breathe a foul or poisonous
atmosphere by which it may be produced. This will lead
him to the study of *atmospheric hygiene*, if we may use
the expression, and he will make the earliest possible
efforts to get rid of noxious gases from his water-closets,
cess-pools, drains, etc.; he will not allow his house to be
pervaded by mouldy and poisonous emanations from his
cellar or basements; nor will he, above all things, allow his
sleeping-rooms to be so confined, that an individual, entering one of them in the morning from the external air, will
be almost instantly made sick. We shall not go into a full
enumeration of those atmospheric abominations, which are
to be found, more or less, in almost every household.

Among the zymotic diseases, as reported by the medical
profession, are carbuncle, cholera-infantum and cholera-

morbus; croup; diarrhœa and dysentery; diphtheria or throat disease; erysipelas; fever and ague; influenza; measles and mumps; puerpural or child-bed fever; quinsey or sore throat; remittent fever; rheumatism; scarlatina, small-pox and varioloid; whooping cough. This is, by no means, a full list of the zymotic diseases. Consumption has been added to the number, and as physicians proceed with their investigations, they may ultimately find that there is scarcely a disease in which foul air, directly or indirectly, has not had something to do in its production.

How then is it possible to recognize the theory of zymotic diseases as true, without recognizing the necessity for ventilation. We must either so construct our houses as to insure within them an adequate supply of pure air, by night as well as by day, or incur the risk of being made dangerously or perhaps fatally sick. In a Report on Zymotic Diseases made to the Massachusetts Medical Society by Dr. Benjamin Cutter, in 1858, he says: "There is no effect without a cause," and adds: "It is well known to every medical practitioner that many persons are, within a short time and within certain limits, affected by the same disease, and that during this time most other diseases partake to a large degree of the nature of the epidemic. The connection between events so common and influences so apparent should excite diligent inquiry, and is a subject of such magnitude and usefulness to mankind that it should command the most serious attention of that body of liberally-educated men who esteem themselves the conservators of the health of the community."

Truthful words, well spoken. But let us not stop with the mere theory of disease, in relation to its exciting causes, but find out, as speedily as possible, how to prevent its development. It will require no prophet, therefore, to tell us that we must cease to breathe foul or poisonous air, as far as possible. This can be prevented by the proper ventilation of our houses; but if the *external air* is impure, in consequence of filth in the streets, imperfect drainage, stagnant pools or marshes, decomposing animal bodies, the contiguity of stables or inclosures in which horses, cows, or swine are kept, or other sources of filth, which are much too common, both in city and country, we must remove the offending cause as quickly as possible, if we would escape the difficulty or danger; or, if we are the inhabitant of a city, we must endeavor to compel the city authorities to enforce a more rigid system of cleansing and purification. When the external air is extremely impure, and becomes stagnant in a house for the want of ventilation, it is doubly poisonous, and can not be breathed a long time without the risk of producing disease or destroying life.

People have no adequate idea how speedily they may become the victims of disease by exposure to a foul air. An hour or two of this exposure may suffice to bring on a fatal malady. The National Hotel Disease, at Washington, is proof of this. There were conflicting theories with regard to the cause of the disease when it first made its appearance, some attributing it to the food, some to the water, and others to the atmosphere, etc. A Dr. Dillard, who was in Washington at the time (vide Transactions of the Philadelphia College of Physicians), testified that a number of his friends who only visited the house, without eating or drinking there, suffered attacks of the epidemic. This goes to show that the limited time devoted to social visits was quite sufficient to engender the disease. Dr. Dillard said further: "The house is a very old one, very much out of repair, decayed and filthy, and I found the odor of its atmosphere so noisome that I got out of it as quickly as I could." With such an explanation as this, no one need be at a loss to comprehend the true cause of the frightful disease in question, by which so many individuals lost their lives, and if people generally would make their escape from foul or pestilential atmospheres as promptly as Dr. Dillard, there would be less sickness, and fewer premature deaths.

The consideration of zymotic diseases suggests the importance of ventilating hospitals, and all institutions designed for the accommodation of invalids. "Hospital gangrene," as it is termed, with erysipelas, and some other diseases peculiar to hospitals, are attributed by the medical profession to foul air, and hence there can be no question about the propriety, not to say absolute necessity, of ventilating hospitals. Thus far, we have not had the satisfaction of ventilating a single hospital.

14

NOXIOUS GASES—HOW THEY ACT UPON AND DESTROY THE
BLOOD—DR. MATTSON'S TESTIMONY.

There are many noxious gases which find their way much too frequently into our breathing atmosphere, as *carbonic acid gas* from the lungs ; *carbonic oxide* from imperfect combustion ; and *carburetted* and *sulphuretted hydrogen* from the decomposition of animal and vegetable matter. The latter gas, so offensive to the smell, is an emanation also from water closets and drains. In further explanation of this subject, I will quote from lectures entitled "Facts for the People concerning Health," etc., by Dr. Morris Mattson, formerly of Boston, but now of New-York City, in which good authority is given for the statement, familiar no doubt to every well-read physician, that sulphuretted hydrogen, and some other gases, will not only darken the blood, but actually decompose it, so that it can not be restored by the oxygen of the air. We can not conceive of any more cogent argument than this in favor of properly ventilating houses, offices, workshops, factories, and all buildings in which human beings are crowded together. We can not do better than to quote a few paragraphs from Dr. Mattson on this important subject. He says :

"*Carburetted* and *sulphuretted hydrogen*, along with *carbonic oxide*, are much to be dreaded when we take into account their peculiar action upon the blood. They produce their effects slowly, but with unerring results, unless the cause be removed. They darken the blood, as does carbonic acid ; but, unlike carbonic acid, they so change its character, that it can not be restored to a healthful condition by oxygen. This is an important consideration. Liebeg says sulphuretted hydrogen turns the globules of the blood blackish-green, and finally black ; and the original red color can not be restored by contact with oxygen, because a decomposition of them has obviously taken place. The globules darkened by carbonic acid, he adds, become again florid in oxygen, and also in nitrous oxide, which shows that they have undergone no decomposition. Here, then, is a difference between the two gases worthy of notice. Lehmann, the great German physiologist, who has the sanction of Professor Samuel Jackson, of the Pennsylvania

University, (*vide* 'Manual of Chemical Physiology,') tells us that 'carbonic oxide and several carbohydrogens' color the blood almost black, and destroy the blood-globules, or, in other words, that they 'combine so firmly with the components of the blood-globules that the previous nature of the blood can in no way be restored.'

"It will be seen, therefore, that the poisonous gases to which we are frequently exposed and obliged to inhale, excepting the carbonic acid, tend directly to decompose or destroy the blood, so that it can never be restored. This is a sufficient explanation of the virulent effects of the gases in question. 'In the blood is the life,' says the inspired volume; and whatever tends to disturb the healthful condition of that fluid must tend directly, and in an equal degree, to disturb the whole system. It need not seem extraordinary, then, that the gases aforesaid, acting suddenly and powerfully upon the system, should, as eminent medical authors allege, produce diarrhœa, dysentery, cholera, typhus, ship and jail fevers, and even the pestilence. But we have these gases frequently in a more dilute form, pervading our kitchens, our parlors, and our sleeping-rooms, and yet, perhaps, not appreciable to the sense of smell. Here, indeed, we have a secret foe, equally unseen and unheeded, which may sap the very foundation of life without our even suspecting the cause. If we become the victims of bad drainage, etc., we constantly inhale those gases while confined within our houses, and they as constantly decompose or destroy our blood. This is especially true at night, while asleep, with perhaps every window carefully and tightly closed, so as to prevent the slightest possible access of pure air. We find ourselves a little pale at first upon rising in the morning, with an unpleasant lassitude, and perhaps some nausea or headache; but we go into the fresh air, and those symptoms are dissipated. In truth, we do not regard them as very important. We renew the inhalations of the poisonous gases, day after day and night after night, until the blood is essentially changed in its healthy composition, and with it the whole system begins to suffer in a marked degree, taking the form of dyspepsia, neuralgia, rheumatism, bilious trouble, heart difficulty, or some other phase of chronic disease. The countenance being pale and haggard,

the doctor prescribes some form of iron, with the hope of
improving the blood, but for some reason or other he finds
he can not produce a favorable change in that fluid. It does
not seem to be understood that the blood is partially decomposed, and that the globules which have suffered this
destruction can never be restored by any human agency ;
nor is *ventilation* thought of as a remedy which, if efficient,
would speedily banish every vestige of the noxious gases
which have caused all the difficulty, and which would prevent any further destruction of the blood-globules—the first
thing, indeed, to be thought of as a curative means. Thus
we are slowly and unconsciously poisoned—poisoned perhaps even unto death. We become the victims of a subtle
agency of which our senses do not take cognizance ; we
yield to a cause of disease which is equally unseen and
unheeded, but which is sure and terrible in its consequences."

PARTICLES FLOATING IN THE ATMOSPHERE.—Mr. J. B.
Dancer recently made a microscopical examination of the
solid particles found in 2,495 litres of the air of Manchester,
England, by Dr. Angus Smith. The air had been washed
in distilled water, and the solid matter which subsided was
collected in a small stoppered bottle. The water containing
the air-washing was first examined by Mr. Dancer with a
power of 50 diameters only, for the purpose of getting a
general knowledge of its contents ; afterward, magnifying
powers varying from 120 to 1,600 diameters were employed.
During the first observations few living organisms were noticed ; but, as it was afterward proved, the germs of plant
and animal life (probably in a dormant condition) were present. Fungoid matter was most abundant. Spores or sporidiæ appeared in numbers, and to ascertain, as nearly as
possible, the numerical proportion of these minute bodies
in a single drop of the fluid, the contents of the bottle were
well shaken, and then one drop was taken up with a pip-
ette ; this was spread out by compression to a circle half an
inch in diameter. A magnifying power was then employed,
which gave a field of view of an area exactly 100th of an
inch in diameter, and it was found that more than 100 spores
were contained in this space ; consequently the average
number of spores in a single drop would be 250,000. These

varied from 10,000th to 50,000th of an inch in diameter.
There were about 150 such drops in the bottle, so that the
sum total of spores reached the startling number of thirty-
seven and a half millions. The mycelium of these minute
fungi were similar to that of rust or mildew (as it is com-
monly named), such as is found on straw or decaying vegetation. When the bottle had remained for 36 hours in a
room at the temperature of 60 degrees the quantity of fungi
was visibly increased, and the delicate, mycelial, thread-like
roots had completely entangled the fibrous objects in the
bottle and formed them into a mass. On the third day a
number of ciliated zoospores were observed moving freely
amongst the sporidiæ. He did not detect any great variety
of fungi in the contents of the bottle ; as there are more than
2,000 different kinds of fungi, it is possible that spores of
other species might have been present, but not under conditions favorable for their development. Some very pretty,
chain-like threads of Conidita were visible in some of the
examinations. The other objects found in the bottle were
vegetable tissue ; brown and charred particles, probably
arising in lighting fires ; a few hairs of the leaves of plants
and fibres ; portions of cotton filaments and of wool, such
as might be expected in the air of a manufacturing city.
A few granules of starch, seen by the aid of the polariscope,
and several long eliptical bodies, similar to the pollen of the
lily, were also noticed. After this dust of the atmosphere
had been kept quiet for three or four days, animalculæ
made their appearance in considerable numbers, the monads
being the most numerous. Animal life soon decreased, and
in twelve days no animalculæ could be detected. The
quantity of air from which all these particles were taken
(2,495 litres, or 549 gallons) is about equal to that which
would be respired in ten hours by a man of ordinary size,
when actively employed. The particles floating in the atmosphere will differ in character according to the season of
the year, the direction of the wind, and the locality in which
they are collected, and, as might be expected, are much less
in quantity after rain.

FOOD OF THE LUNGS—ATMOSPHERIC IMPURITIES, ETC.—
People are usually very particular, and sometimes almost
dainty, in reference to their food and drink, but they seldom

give much attention to the *food of their lungs*—the *food*, it may be said, *of the blood itself*—which should consist of pure, uncontaminated air, with its full supply of vitalizing oxygen. The food of the lungs, therefore, is even more important than the food of the stomach. An individual may indignantly reject his bread and butter, or his pudding, because it contains a mote, and at the same time take into his lungs, from the atmosphere, the most disgusting impurities of which it is possible to conceive, although they may not be apparent to the senses.

Indeed, the atmosphere is constantly loaded with impurities to an almost incredible extent, and is therefore an abundant source of disease. We find in it carbonic acid, ammonia, carburetted and sulphuretted hydrogen, carbonic oxide, the malarious poisons, and certain poisons which are evolved from the human body, and from all animal organisms. We may add to these the various poisons used in manufacturing purposes, which tend to produce disease or depress the powers of life, and also the ever-present *tobacco smoke*, which is blown from the mouths of smokers, loaded with effluvia from rotten teeth, or ulcerated gums and throats. The tobacco nuisance may be obviated within doors by having ventilated smoking rooms, which are spoken of in another place.

Where any or all of the poisons here enumerated are unduly concentrated in our breathing atmosphere, especially during night in our sleeping apartments, the health will gradually give way, or sudden attacks of disease will be produced, which may prove dangerous or fatal.

Even horses become blind, or diseased, and that not unfrequently, in consequence of impure air in their stables; and it is now sufficiently notorious that cows, shut up in stables with inadequate ventilation, furnish milk of a poisonous character, which no doubt adds materially to our mortality, especially among children.

All of the evils flowing from an impure or tainted atmosphere may be remedied by our system of ventilation, as will be seen by reference to the numerous testimonials which have been received from many distinguished individuals.

FOUL AIR AND DISEASE SYNONYMOUS.

The writer of this is not a physician, but in the course of his professional duties, ventilating kitchens, basements, water-closets, offices, stables, and all sorts of places, he has seen enough to satisfy him that a great deal of disease results from bad air without the cause oftentimes being suspected. The people have yet to learn that pure air is one of the most essential requisites of a healthy existence. The influence of bad air has been constantly apparent to the writer. He recently visited a poor-house, in which there was no adequate ventilation, and the children were nearly all suffering with sore eyes and other marks of disease. They were wretched-looking objects. The directors feared the approach of cholera, and wished to have the place ventilated. When this is done, it will be found that much of the prevailing disease will disappear.

We ventilated a large banking-house in New York City in which the air was extremely foul, and, when the work was done, the clerks experienced an immediate change in the atmosphere; they felt refreshed and invigorated, instead of experiencing that sense of weariness and lassitude which accompanies a noxious air. One of the clerks, who had been for a long time asthmatic, immediately recovered his health.

A gentleman occupying a very handsome residence, had what he considered a damp and unwholesome parlor, for he scarcely ever came home from his counting-room and threw himself upon the sofa without feeling as though he had taken a severe cold. Underneath the parlor was a damp sub-cellar, to which the writer attributed the difficulty, and, upon establishing a proper ventilation, he ceased to take cold, and ceased also to be troubled with attacks of rheumatic pains.

Not only man but the domestic animals suffer from impure air. We have frequently noticed this in ventilating horse stables. The poor animals, not having a full supply of pure air, gradually sicken, and begin to lose their sight. There is an immense amount of blindness among horses on this account. It does not seem to be understood that a horse needs fresh air quite as much as he needs hay or oats. We have seen splendid horses, which have cost the owners several thousand dollars apiece, sold at auction for a mere song on account of blindness, induced by being shut up in close stables.

SLEEPY CONGREGATIONS—SERMON ON THE MOUNT—ST. PAUL —REV. ROBERT COLLYER—WESLEY AND WHITEFIELD— BY MORRIS MATTSON, M. D.

With regard to sleeping in church, it seems to be a question whether it is an *asphyxia*, or a mere somnolent condition resulting from dull and tedious sermons. We are a convert to the doctrine of asphyxia, not knowing why the excess of carbonic acid and other poisons, which accumulate in churches devoid of ventilation, should not put people to sleep as effectually as the carbonic acid from a charcoal furnace in a close room. The only wonder is, that any body can keep awake in a crowded and unventilated church. We are sure, therefore, that this tendency to sleep is not to be attributed to dull sermons. With fresh air to breathe during church services, it would be almost as impossible to go to sleep as it would be in walking by the sea-side or upon the mountain top. We have made these remarks with the view of quoting what the Rev. Robert Collyer says upon the subject of sleepy congregations, as he ought to be considered good authority. He is charitable in his views, and expresses himself as follows: "This may be one of those things in which nobody is to blame, except as we are to blame for any other sickness. The preacher has written too many sermons, and the people have heard too many for ten months past. They want a vacation all round." He then quotes Dean Ramsey as telling a story of an old Scotch minister who one Sunday saw his whole congregation asleep, except an idiot in the gallery. He stopped, and his people all woke up, and then he cried, "Are you not ashamed to be asleep as I preach the Word, while that poor idiot is broad awake?" "Deed, minister," the fool replied, "if I had na been an idiot I wad 'a been asleep too."

A good excuse for what may be considered a bad habit is well enough now and then; at all events it shows a benevolent spirit on the part of the reverend and distinguished gentleman from whom we have quoted. Nevertheless, it would be better to strike at the root of the evil, and insist upon churches being ventilated. The history of religion proves that it thrives the best in pure air, as we shall show presently. An eminent clergyman has said that it is a sin to be sick, and if this be true, it is a sin to visit some of our fashionable churches, for by so doing one is almost sure to contract a headache, or some other corporeal affliction, such as usually ensues from breathing a poisonous or unwholesome atmosphere Foul air is the very antipodes of religion. It deadens the faculties of the mind, and weakens the devotional feelings The human brain is a species of galvanic battery, which works the best when stimulated by pure air. The spiritual power of the Apostles was no doubt intensified by their out-of-door life and preaching. Had they preached exclusively in the synagogues — assuming that the synagogues were no better ventilated than our modern churches— they would have had fewer proselytes. .   .   . Leaving the Apostolic Age, and coming down to the seventeenth century, we find John Wesley and George Whitefield, in imitation of the Apostles, preaching in the open air, and exercising a potent influence upon the public mind. They performed herculean labors, as men usually do who work in the open air and bright sunshine. Mr. Wesley, not waiting for churches to be built, preached to out-of-door audiences wherever he could find them, and by this practice his health was promoted and his life prolonged. He lived to be eighty-eight years old, notwithstanding a somewhat delicate constitution. Mr. Whitefield, at one time the co-laborer of Wesley, also devoted himself to open-air preaching. In England, Wales, and Scotland, according to his biographer, he preached to immense crowds, and always in the open air. He has stated in some personal memoranda, that during a period of thirty-four years of his ministry, he preached upwards of 18,000 sermons, crossed the Atlantic seven times, and traveled thousands of miles both in Britain and America. When his strength began to fail, he put himself on what he termed "short allowance," preaching but once daily during the week, and three times on the Sabbath. He ultimately gave up his labors in the open air for the pulpit of a non-ventilated church in Portsmouth, New Hampshire, where he caught cold and died. Had he confined himself to open-air preaching, his life would no doubt have been prolonged.

We learn from those retrospections that fresh air is the very handmaid of religion. If we were seeking to bring about a great religious revival, we would begin by ventilating the churches. Fresh air is essential to health and physical power, and, without these, the manifestation of spiritual power will be more or less deficient. If we compel a Minister of the Gospel to preach in an unventilated church, and, withal, oblige him to live and sleep in an unventilated house, it will not be easy for him to escape some form of invalidism, unless he should have the physical system of a Martin Luther. Thus, his power of doing good, or of making a religious impression upon the minds of his hearers, will be greatly diminished.

The open-air preaching of the Apostles, and of John Wesley and George Whitefield, remind us of the sermon on the Mount, which was also delivered in the open air—the pure mountain air—and it was the best sermon ever preached. We venture to say that not one of the great multitude of people coming from Gallilee, and Jerusalem, and Judea, who listened to that sermon, fell asleep, or was even troubled with drowsiness. Not so however with the preaching of St. Paul in the close, unventilated loft, described in the Acts of the Apostles. That the place was unventilated, we take for granted. The scriptural version is this : "And there sat in a window a certain young man, being fallen into a deep sleep : and as Paul was long preaching, he sunk down with sleep, and fell down from the third loft, and was taken up dead." He was not dead, however. St. Paul said, "Trouble not yourselves, for the life is still in him." The young man was afterward restored to life, and it is to be presumed that he only fainted or swooned, or, to use a modern word, was *asphixiated*, as people are daily asphixiated in our churches, and other crowded places. But, says a critical person, the young man was seated in a window, and could not have been put to sleep by the foul air. Nay, just the reverse of this. When a window, connected with a warm, unventilated room, is open, two currents of air may be observed, one, which is the cooler, passing in at the bottom, and the other, which is warmer, passing out at the top. We infer that the window was low, and that the young man was exposed to the upper current. This being the case, he was compelled to breathe the foul air of the loft in its most concentrated form. He was in more danger of being asphixiated in this outward current than the people within the enclosure, where the poison of the atmosphere was less intense. St. Paul had, no doubt, often observed such cases. Saying, as he did, that the life still remained in the young man, it is to be inferred that he had often seen his followers go to sleep in a similar way, when he was obliged to preach in close places, devoid of ventilation. The Apostles, therefore, when preaching within doors, had the same difficulties to encounter in respect to vitiated atmospheres that clergymen have to encounter at the present day. But the Apostles were excusable, because science, at that remote period, had made but little progress, and the discovery of oxygen and carbonic acid had not been made. We can offer no such plea at present. We are no longer excusable on the ground of ignorance. We boast of our scientific knowledge; we know all about the composition of the air—all about oxygen and carbonic acid; and we teach chemistry, physiology, and other sciences to the boys and girls in our common schools, having much to say in reference to the importance of pure air, but not allowing the pupils to have any pure air to breathe. Our science, therefore, is like a crab—it goes backward instead of forward.

If the word *asphyxia* is not plain to the common reader, we will save him the trouble of hunting up his dictionary. It signifies an interruption of the breathing process. There are several varieties of it, one of which is termed *asphyxia mephitica*, indicating that condition which results from breathing *choke-damp*. This phrase, in its turn, may need an explanation. The miners call any irrespirable gas or vapor, "choke-damp." Carbonic acid gas, in particular, comes within this definition. We have plenty of choke-damp in our churches and other public places.

Speaking of the poisonous effect of the outward current of air which asphixiated the young man mentioned by St. Paul, it is well to remember that it is always dangerous to breathe any heated current of air which has been poisoned by the human breath. A melancholy case of the kind is recalled to our memory. We refer to an estimable lady who died suddenly from the noxious air of a crowded church. Strangers had occupied her pew in the body of the church, and not wishing to disturb them she made her way to a front seat in the gallery, directly over a gas-jet. The heat of this jet established an up-moving current of air, which came directly into her face, bringing with it the concentrated miasms and poisons of the church-atmosphere. This poison was too potent for the unfortunate lady. She went home complaining of illness. A doctor was called. His treatment seemed to be of no avail. She rapidly failed in strength. The physician was unable to give any name to her disease, for her symptoms were strange and anomalous. Death, however, soon made sure of its victim, and she passed from time to eternity. A valuable life was here lost, which was a loss to society as well as to the family circle; and it is not too much to say, that while the Church is seeking to save the souls of men and women, it should be careful not to destroy their bodies.

Persons of a delicate organization, or those who are easily disturbed by external influences, are the most likely to suffer from the noxious air of a church, or other crowded place, and should therefore be extremely careful how they expose themselves to this source of danger.

CHURCHES—A NEW MODE OF VENTILATION TESTED—ANEC-
DOTE OF A DISTINGUISHED CLERGYMAN.

If it is not desirable for people to go to sleep during divine service, then it is important to ventilate your churches. It is not always dull sermons that make people drowsy; it is much more frequently the foul air of a church, which deadens all the faculties of the mind, and induces that drowsy condition, so unpleasant to the individual, and yet so difficult to be overcome. Sleepiness in church and in other public places, in which human beings are densely packed together, is not dissimilar, in many instances, from the sleepiness and stupor induced by breathing the carbonic acid gas emitted from a charcoal furnace in a close room. The lungs of the auditors are indeed so many charcoal furnaces, throwing out every instant copious volumes of carbonic acid gas; and as churches are seldom or never ventilated, it is no wonder that people go to sleep. The only wonder is, that they do not frequently go to sleep never again to wake ; and it will yet be found and acknowledged, by those who investigate hygienic and sanitary laws, that human life is frequently shortened by a slow and gradual process of poisoning, induced by the noxious air of churches and other public places.

It is my privilege, I trust, though I do not do it with any captious spirit, to speak of a well-known church in which a new experiment in ventilation was tried. And, by the way, if ever a church needed ventilation, it was that one. It is densely crowded, particularly in the evenings ; and if any one wishes to know how much *bad air* he can inhale in the course of two hours, without undergoing positive suffocation or asphyxia, he has only to make an evening visit to said church. The Board of Trustees finally concluded that a little less carbonic acid gas, and a little more pure, fresh air, would be a desideratum ; and, in accordance with that wise decision, they agreed to avail themselves of the services of an educated and distinguished gentleman, who had introduced a new mode of ventilation, which was highly applauded by some of our popular journals. Explanations were made by him to those interested ; plans were drawn upon paper ; and everything pertaining to the new method seemed to promise entire success. The experiment was duly undertaken ; a large number of men were employed ; the parties worked diligently for three months, and, as a matter of course, used up a large amount of money. Unfortunately, however, for some unexpected reason, the experiment did not work well, and the enterprise was finally suspended, never again to be resumed.

Anxious to learn the particulars of the above experiment, and accidentally meeting the distinguished pastor of the church, with whom I had not the pleasure of an acquaintance, I nevertheless took the liberty of interrogating him upon the subject. Pausing for a moment, he made this sententious, emphatic, and characteristic reply, the words of which I can put on paper, but without giving any idea of the peculiar inflections of his voice, or the curious blending, as it seemed to me, of the humor and pathos which he infused into his answer. He said, "They have been at work *three months*, they have expended *three thousand dollars,** and they have not got fresh air enough into the church to feed *three flies.*"

Let this church be properly ventilated, and the noted pastor, though he may not be more eloquent and impassioned, will be likely to add ten years to his pastoral life. Constant dropping, it is said, will wear out a stone ; and so the breathing of foul air, at frequent intervals, along with great physical and mental effort, can not fail to make an ultimate impression even upon the healthful and vigorous system of the pastor in question. It was found that the soldiers in the English barracks, near London, in consequence of imperfect ventilation, did not live as long by ten years, upon an average, as the agricultural population, outside of the barracks, under similar conditions of life, excepting that they had a pure and wholesome air.

WATER-CLOSET VENTILATION.

Many of our finest houses are rendered almost intolerable by the water-closets, the foul odors of which may be detected from the basement to the attic, and yet the remedy is perfectly simple and easily applied. The unwholesome odors and gases may be readily exchanged for the sweet, pure air. In my mode of ventilating water-closets, the foul air *beneath* the seat is made to ascend through a flue, by means of a rarified atmosphere, carrying with it cigar smoke, or other disagreeable odors *above* the seat, or within the inclosure or apartment in which the closet is located ; and thus the mingled impurities of the atmosphere, so offensive to the sense of smell, and so injurious to the health, are scattered upon the wings of the wind. I have ventilated numerous closets for our wealthy families, and always to their great delight and satisfaction.

SMOKING-ROOMS—REGARD FOR THE HEALTH OF YOUR WIFE AND FAMILY.

These should always be ventilated, whether they exist in public places or private houses. Even the accustomed smoker would be better not to inhale over and over again the smoke emitted from his cigar or pipe. Nor is the idea a

* The sum actually expended was $5,000.

very pleasant one of taking into one's lungs the tobacco smoke which proceeds from the mouth of another, mingled usually with an offensive breath, and not unfrequently the noxious effluvia from ulcerated gums and decaying teeth. No true gentleman, who seeks the indulgence of his cigar, will allow himself to inflict the smoke upon others who may regard it as a nuisance. Hence, ventilation is necessary ; and in that case you may smoke your cigar in the presence of your wife or daughter, or some anti-tobacco friend, without creating a feeling of unpleasantness or disgust. Where smoking-rooms are not ventilated, the paper upon the walls, the furniture, and every thing within the room, become saturated with the smoke, and are rendered very disagreeable. Many fine houses have been ruined by excessive cigar smoking, as the walls and wood-work retain the tobacco odor for a long period. Besides, your dresses become so tainted by the smoke as to render you disagreeable, in many instances, to ladies and gentlemen seated near you in cars, omnibuses, and public places. Every consideration then of refinement and delicacy, with a due regard for the comfort, well-being, and health of those about you, should either prompt you to give up the habit of smoking or to have your apartments ventilated so as to conduct the smoke quickly away. Even the health of your wife may suffer from the poisonous effects of your cigar ; and yet she may not complain, as she does not wish to deprive you of any of your enjoyments. Rooms ventilated by my process are at once freed from the smoke, as well as any other impurity in the atmosphere, so that there is no taint nor disagreeable odor left behind.

FACTS CONCERNING THE PRESERVATION OF MEAT, BUTTER, AND MILK—VENTILATED MILK AND BUTTER HOUSES— TESTIMONY OF MRS. G. S. ROBBINS.

It is a curious fact that fresh meat, suddenly frozen, will undergo a destructive change in its central or interior parts, so as to be unfit for use. Dr. Kane mentions a similar fact as taking place in the Arctic regions, with the thermometer fifty or sixty degrees below zero. The walrus and other meats, which he was enabled to obtain in those high latitudes, freezing suddenly, underwent decomposition in the interior, greatly to his surprise, and could not be used as food. The pork-packers acknowledge the loss of pork, now and then, from a similar cause. I know of but one explanation of the phenomenon. The frozen crust of the meat is probably impervious to the gases of the interior, so that they can not escape, and decomposition ensues precisely in the same way that fresh meat decomposes or putrifies in a close, unventilated refrigerator, notwithstanding the presence of the ice. One thing at least is very apparent, namely, that in preserving fresh meat we need something more than a cold atmosphere; and I have elsewhere stated that in my ventilated refrigerators a temperature of only fifty degrees is all that is required for the preservation of fresh meat.

In contrast with the facts above stated, it is equally curious that in some sections of our country, and also in some parts of Mexico, fresh meat hung up in the open air, without any salt, even in the hot weather of summer, will not undergo any unfavorable change, but gradually dry up and remain fit for food. One explanation is, that certain prevailing winds sweep away all of the gases exhaled by the meat as fast as they appear, so that there are no noxious agencies remaining by which the meat can be decomposed.

There is a curious fact, also, in relation to milk, the interior portion of which frequently becomes sour, while the exterior portions continue sweet. This change takes place, notwithstanding the milk may be placed in a cold refrigerator, and the change occurs more speedily when the vessel containing the milk is closely covered. This difficulty in relation to milk has induced many of our citizens to apply to me for ventilated milk-houses, which they have used with much satisfaction, and which should have a place in every hotel, restaurant, and private family.

Butter, as well as milk, is extremely sensitive to the influence of a pent-up and foul atmosphere, such as we usually find in refrigerators. A foul or strong odor will taint the very best butter in a few hours. Those who are using my *ventilated butter-houses* and *refrigerators* have no trouble in keeping their butter sweet and good for a long period of time.

With regard to the preservation of milk, I might quote several authorities, but will content myself with that of the well-known Mrs. G. S. Robbins, who deserves so well of her country for the noble services which she has rendered to our suffering soldiers at the McDougall Hospital at Fort Schuyler. One of my large refrigerators was placed in the hospital through her influence, and after the use of it for six months in connection with the "Ladies' Kitchen" she says: "It is certainly a most admirable invention, enabling us to keep, in the most perfect preservation, during the unusual heat of the past summer, *milk*, poultry, meats, fruits, vegetables, etc., with, as I have frequently heard the steward remark, a very economical consumption of ice."

THE FOOD WE EAT—VENTILATED PROVISION CLOSETS.

This is a subject deserving more care and attention than it usually receives. We not only poison our blood with foul air, but frequently also by the use of improper food. The noxious gases which are so detrimental to the life forces, when taken into the lungs, will also, retained in refrigerators and provision closets, produce rapid putrefactive changes in the meat, fruits, and other articles of food which may be present. Food may be rendered unwholesome indepently of a change which would be perceptible to the sense of smell. Carry off the noxious gases in question, however, as rapidly as they are formed, which is done in my *ventilated provision closets*, and it will be found that our most perishable fruits, of which strawberries are a good type, will be preserved in a sound condition for ten days or longer, and fresh meat will keep sweet and good in the hot weather of summer for several weeks, retaining in the mean time its natural red color. Nothing will explain better than this, to the popular mind, the baneful effects of noxious airs and gases, not only in hastening destructive changes in our food, but in deteriorating or destroying our health. Hence it is that a cheap and efficient system of ventilation is one of the great needs of the age—one of the most urgent wants of our social system.

FRUIT ROOMS—PRESERVATION OF FRUIT IN ITS NATURAL STATE — STRAWBERRIES KEPT TEN DAYS, AND RIPE PEACHES THREE WEEKS.

Millions of money are expended annually in the cultivation and perfection of fruit, which is becoming almost a mania with many of our fruit-growers; and out of this has arisen a heavy and profitable business in fruit.

Fruit-rooms are needed by all dealers in fruit, by the keepers of hotels and restaurants, by exporters of fruit, and by families who purchase fruit in considerable quantities as a luxury. The fruit thus accumulated is worth hundreds and frequently thousands of dollars, and as it is extremely liable to perish, it is important to improve the method by which it can be preserved. What is required for this purpose is a pure dry air, and the instant abstraction, as soon as it appears, of every noxious gas, along with a properly regulated temperature—all of which conditions are furnished by my mode of ventilation. Strawberries, which are the most perishable of all the fruits, have been kept in a good condition for ten days, and ripe peaches for three weeks. These experiments have been made repeatedly, and particularly by Mr. David Tilton, of Tompkins Market, so that there can be no doubt of the correctness of my statement.

Mr. Tilton was so well pleased with his success in preserving perishable fruits, that he employed me to construct a *fruit-house* for him on board of the steamer Liberty, Capt. Wilson, about to sail for Havana, for the purpose of exporting peaches and pears to that city. Let it be here understood that three quarters of the peaches and pears forwarded to Havana, although packed in ice with great care, perish before their arrival at that port. I constructed a house for Mr. Tilton in the hold of the vessel, (the last place that would be dreamed of for the preservation of delicate and perishable fruits,) large enough to receive four hundred baskets of peaches and Bartlett pears. The fruit was duly put on board, but with the belief of every body but Mr. Tilton and myself that but few if any of the peaches and pears would ever arrive in a sound condition at their place of destination. This opinion was regarded as all the more plausible because the fruit was in the hold of the vessel, where we expect to find the odor of bilge water and various noxious gases. The vessel sailed, and in nine days the fruit was taken out of the house in which it had been inclosed, and with the exception of about a peck of peaches in close proximity with the ventilating pipe, it was found in a perfect condition, and according to Mr. Mills, the steward (who, by the way, had prophesied that not a single peach or pear would ever reach Havana in a sound state), it could have been returned to New York in an equally good condition. The secret of this desirable preservation of fruit lies chiefly in the ready abstraction from the fruit-chamber of dampness and every noxious gas, which, if permitted to remain, would cause the speedy destruction of the fruit.

REFRIGERATORS.

Refrigerators of the smaller sizes abound in the market, and are purchased largely by families on account of their cheapness. Some of them claim to be ventilated, but it is in a very limited degree, and consequently articles of food can not be preserved in them for a long period. Every refrigerator, whether large or small, should be *perfectly ventilated*, whereby all the noxious or unwholesome gases which are constantly forming are carried off, and pure, dry, cold air furnished in their place. It is only under these conditions that food is wholesome or fit to be eaten; for if foul air is allowed to accumulate in the refrigerator, it will be absorbed by the food, and its healthful qualities more or less impaired. It is the presence of this foul air which causes food to undergo decomposition, rendering it thereby unfit for use.

Refrigerators of a small size may be ventilated by my method; but I do not pretend to furnish them to the public. Refrigerators on a large scale, however, together with fruit and provision-closets and meat-houses, I am always ready to construct to order, and I have no evidence that they can be thoroughly and efficiently ventilated excepting by the plan which I have secured by my letters patent.

The air is always pure, sweet, and dry in my ventilated refrigerators; and I have stated elsewhere that fresh meat will keep within them, during the hot weather of summer, for three weeks, and retain in the mean time its red color; strawberries will keep ten days; ripe peaches and delicate pears will keep three weeks, or longer, and so on to the end of a long chapter. The odor of one kind of food, however strong, will not be imparted to any other, because the odors and gases, as already explained, are not retained sufficiently long to undergo absorption by the provisions present.

PORK-HOUSE VENTILATION — MESSRS. SILVERHORN, MILLE-
MANN, AND LOCKETT—PORK CURED AT FIFTY DEGREES
OF TEMPERATURE.

A large proportion of the people of the United States,
having no special regard for the old Mosaic law, are great
lovers of pork, and consequently the pork business is a
thriving and profitable branch of trade. This presupposes
the necessity of pork-houses for curing and preserving
the meat, and as the dealers frequently have from twenty to
one hundred thousand dollars of their stock on hand at a
time, the question of perfect ventilation is an important one,
especially as thousands of dollars worth of the meat is liable
to spoil in a very short time.

One of my earliest experiments in ventilation was for Mr.
Silverhorn, in New York City, in 1862, who conducted a
large pork-curing establishment. By reference to his card
at the end of this volume it will be seen that the experiment was successful. The foul and damp atmosphere of his
cooling-rooms was replaced by one perfectly dry and pure ;
his men ceased to complain of sickness ; and he found his
pork would cure as well in summer, with the aid of my ventilating process, as it had done in winter at a temperature of
thirty-eight or thirty-nine degrees. I may add that there
has been no instance of pork going into one of my ventilated houses in a sound and sweet condition that was not
found equally sound and sweet when taken out.

In 1863, I ventilated the pork-house of Mr. Millemann,
who had been in the business forty years, and who had ample experience with regard to the various methods of cooling
and ventilating pork-houses. Observing the thermometer
as high as fifty degrees under my direction, he became very
much alarmed, as he had $40,000 worth of pork on hand,
and he had been accustomed to as low a temperature as
thirty-eight or forty degrees. He found, however, that his
pork cured better at fifty degrees than it had ever done with
lower temperatures by the old methods. [See his card in
another place.]

It will be seen, therefore, that I use much less ice than is
necessary in the old method. The most experienced dealers

in pork deemed it requisite to have a temperature in their pork-houses of about thirty-six or thirty-eight degrees, but certainly never exceeding forty degrees; and when I proposed to employ a temperature of only fifty degrees, every one of them seemed to regard it with extreme skepticism. Hence it will be seen that it is the lack of ventilation in the old method which hastens the destruction of the meat, and that by ventilating efficiently, so as to carry off the foul air rapidly, the pork may be cured and preserved at a much higher temperature.

PARAN STEVENS, ESQ. — VENTILATION OF HIS STABLE, KITCHEN, AND REFRIGERATOR — MEAT-HOUSE IN THE FIFTH AVENUE HOTEL.

The late Paran Stevens is well known as the Napoleon of popular hotels in the United States. A. B. Darling, Esq., one of his partners in the *Fifth Avenue Hotel*, is also a representative man, though not so extensively known to the public as Mr. Stevens. He arranged the general plan and construction of the hotel, and is its chief manager, purchasing all the provisions and stores used in the establishment. In that capacity he applied to me for my services in ventilating his *meat-house*. When the hotel was first commenced, he used large provision closets or refrigerators, with the ordinary but wholly inadequate ventilation. These were soon abandoned, because it was found that the meats speedily spoiled. He then packed his meats in large chests, alternating with layers of ice, which preserved the meats a longer time; but it was found that the portions of the meat in contact with the ice would be bleached perfectly white, and had to be cut off and thrown away. This, of course, was a great loss. Nevertheless, this plan was continued for many years, until I constructed for him a large ventilated meat-house, capable of holding one or two tons of meat, which he has used ever since. With a temperature not exceeding forty-five or fifty degrees, he can keep meat in the hottest days of summer as long as he desires, which is usually a week or ten days; and during this time it retains its red color, which indicates that it is in the best and most wholesome condition for food. I am assured that not a pound of meat has been lost since the meat-house was put into operation. It is with some little professional pride and pleasure, therefore, that I would suggest to a generous public, not already familiar with the culinary and other attractions of the Fifth Avenue Hotel, that if they are desirous of regaling their palates with the best and choicest meats which the market affords, they need only record their names as guests at the above celebrated house. Indeed, it may be confidently stated that meats kept for a period of about ten days, (this is the theory of Mr. Darling,) in one of my ventilated meat-houses or provision closets, whereby they have no opportunity of absorbing the injurious gases constantly present in close or imperfectly ventilated refrigerators, have a savory richness and delicacy, and withal a nutritive quality, not characteristic of meats kept in the ordinary way.

Succeeding so well in the experiment with the meat-house, Mr. Darling employed me to ventilate all of his provision rooms, and also the large water-closet of the hotel. which had caused a great deal of trouble, and was a source of discomfort to the guests.

With this favorable introduction into the establishment, I was requested to call upon Mr. Stevens, whose name is at the head of this article, and who had been complaining for a considerable time of the inadequate ventilation of his horse stable, perceiving, when he entered it, a stifling atmosphere and an almost intolerable odor, which was even perceptible in his horses when they were brought into the open air; and withal, his horses appeared to be in an unhealthy condition, with cold ears, bloodshot eyes, and other signs of disease. It was under these circumstances that Mr. Stevens wished to avail himself of my new system of ventilation, for he had hitherto looked in vain for any relief from the troubles enumerated above. I found in his stable five splendid horses, for one of which he had recently paid five thousand dollars. The stable I found to be almost destitute of ventilation, notwithstanding an ample flue put up at the head of each stall in the original construction of the building, and which the architect, without doubt, deemed all-sufficient for the purposes of ventilation. There was also, in addition to the flues, a large trap or ventilator in the skylight ; but, with all of these contrivances, the atmosphere in the stable was of the most offensive character, and the poor horses, valued at a little fortune, were suffering for the want of a due supply of that indispensable element of life and health, pure air. I proceeded at once to ventilate the stable, and in a few weeks after the work was completed, I called upon Mr. Stevens to inquire what had been the result of the experiment. He assured me that it had worked splendidly, and that his stable now abounded with a pure, sweet and wholesome air. A great lover of that noble animal, the horse, as Mr. Stevens is known to be, I could not but observe the pleasure which he manifested in having been able to improve the sanitary condition of his favorite animals.

Deriving so much satisfaction from the introduction of a pure atmosphere into his stable, Mr. Stevens now had his attention recalled very forcibly to the sad condition of his kitchen, which, he said, abounded in offensive and unwholesome odors, and which, as is common in all similar cases, were constantly pervading the rooms above, and rendering his parlors, his art-gallery, and other apartments extremely disagreeable. A ventilator, so called, had been placed in the flue, extending up from the kitchen, but it proved to be of no avail ; and he had almost decided to tear down this flue and erect another in its place, extending to the height of five stories, with the hope that the defects herein described might be obviated. He was gratified to find, however, that instead of an expenditure of five or six thousand dollars, which a new flue would cost, he could have his kitchen ventilated by my simple method at comparatively little expense. The work was commenced and speedily completed, and I had the assurance of Mr. Stevens that the experiment was entirely successful, and that he was no longer troubled with an impure or disagreeable atmosphere in his private apartments.

Mr. Stevens next desired me to ventilate a large refrigerator, which he used for private purposes, and into which choice meats, game, and other provisions were placed for preservation. As he had become somewhat accustomed to the pleasures of a sweet atmosphere in his stable, kitchen and private parlors, he had no difficulty in detecting the very impure atmosphere which pervaded this refrigerator.

Indeed, upon opening the door, the air was almost sickening, and the idea of a dinner of sirloin or canvas-back from such a receptacle was anything but agreeable. And here it ought to be borne in mind that no food is fit to be eaten which is confined a long time in such an atmosphere as here described. The provisions are tainted by the noxious gases which are present, and these gases, as already stated, are regarded by physicians as more or less poisonous to the blood and the whole system. Mr. Stevens was not to be censured for this sad condition of his private larder, for he knew not how to remedy the evil, and a peep into the refrigerators of our fashionable hotels, boarding-houses, and private dwellings will frequently disclose an odor not at all suggestive of "Sweet-brier" or "Verbena." Some months after ventilation had been established in the above refrigerator, I was informed that not a pound of meat, poultry, nor game had been lost since the experiment was commenced, whereas previously many of the articles put into it had been spoiled.

In due time I called upon Mr. Stevens to ascertain whether my labors in his behalf had proved satisfactory, and if so, whether he would favor me with a letter setting forth this fact to the public. Without any reserve, he replied : "Certainly, with great pleasure, because you are doing good to the public, and it is my duty to inform the public of the services which you are capable of rendering them. If I were not lame," added Mr. Stevens, "I would go about and advertise you myself."

VENTILATION OF STABLES—HORSES SICKEN AND DIE FROM BAD AIR—ZOÖLOGICAL GARDENS—VARNISH OF CARRIAGES DESTROYED—COW STABLES—POISONOUS MILK—STATEMENT BY PROFESSOR DOREMUS.

The ventilation of stables intended for the accommodation of our domestic animals, and especially the horse, is a matter of very great importance. It is claimed by those who have had ample experience, that there are more horses dying annually from imperfect ventilation than all other causes combined. Bad air is known to produce blindness in horses, which is becoming very prevalent, especially in

New-York City, where horses are often crowded together in very small stables. A horse is frequently valued at five or ten thousand dollars, and sometimes more, and it is surprising that the owner of so valuable and noble an animal should ever endanger its health or life for the want of proper ventilation, which would cost but a trifling comparative sum. A horse, with its large, vigorous lungs, requires a large amount of fresh air, which it is impossible for it to obtain in a close or badly ventilated stable, especially when several animals are crowded together in a small space. The horse then begins to droop and show signs of disease; his ears grow cold; his eyes lose their brilliancy, and finally his sight becomes impaired; his step becomes less firm and elastic; and when he is taken from the stable, it is not until he has had time to take in copious draughts of fresh air, that he begins to brighten up or manifest his usual vigor and animation. A horse is almost as susceptible to the influence of fresh air as a human being is to that of laughing gas, and in proportion as he is deprived of it, in that proportion will his health and usefulness be impaired, even though his life may not be destroyed.

A brother of mine in Boston, some years ago, had a valuable horse which became sick in consequence, as it was believed, of a poorly ventilated stable. His life being despaired of, it was arranged to send him to a veterinary surgeon in Cambridge, just across the river from Boston, for treatment. Three men were employed to conduct the animal to his new quarters, one to lead him, and the other two to support him on either side, as he was liable, from his great exhaustion, to stagger and fall to the ground. The bridge by which the river is crossed was finally gained, and here the horse appeared to be reviving under the influence of the pure air sweeping across the bridge. His step was gradually becoming more firm and elastic, but all at once he came to a sudden pause, and threw up his head as if some new element of life had been infused into his veins. He stood quietly in this position for several minutes, with an appearance of delight and pleasure, and seemed to be instinctively taking into his lungs full draughts of the fresh air which he had so much needed, and which so revived him that in a short time he proceeded over the bridge with a vigorous step, without any support from the men in attendance. Let it not be forgotten, then, that fresh air is just as important to a horse as his food or drink.

"The effects of air vitiated by animal effluvia," says Mr. Tomlinson, in his "Rudimentary Treatise on Warming and Ventilation," "are evident in the diseases of the lower animals when crowded together in confined places. The glanders of horses, the pip of fowls, and a peculiar disease in sheep, all arise from this cause; and it is stated that, for some years past, the English nation has been saved £10,000 a year in consequence of the army veterinary surgeons adopting a plan for the ventilation of the cavalry stables."

The same writer quotes the well-known Dr. Arnott, who alludes to the want of knowledge among all classes on the subject of ventilation, and states that he had heard at the Zoological Gardens of a class of animals where fifty out of sixty were killed in a month from putting them into a house which had no opening in it but a few inches in the floor. It is pointedly added that this was like putting the animals under an extinguisher.

A noted lawyer of New York City, whose name I do not feel at liberty to publish, solicited me to ventilate his stables, saying that he had just sold, or more properly given away, a pair of horses for which he had recently paid $6000, in consequence of their sight becoming so much impaired as to render them nearly useless. He attributed the disaster to imperfect ventilation, but did not know how to remedy the difficulty. He had employed a leading architect to ventilate his art gallery, library, kitchen, etc., but his efforts were fruitless, and he was very zealous in the hope that I might produce better results by my improved system of ventilation.

I have ventilated a great many stables belonging to the wealthy citizens of New York City, and always with entire success. The atmosphere of those stables is generally stifling and offensive in a marked degree, and that horses confined within them should become blind, or sicken and die, need not excite our wonder. When stables are properly ventilated, the air within them is always sweet and wholesome, and the horses or other animals which they may contain are in no danger of losing their health or lives.

There is another reason why horse stables should be ventilated. The air within them is charged with ammoniacal vapor, which is not only injurious to horses, but tends to destroy the paint and varnish on carriages in a very short time. I have ventilated stables from this consideration alone, having no reference to the health of the horses.

Cow Stables.—These, as well as horse stables, should be well ventilated, for milk is an indispensable article of food, and no cow can furnish wholesome milk if she is forced to breathe a foul or contaminated air. We need not expect to find pure milk where we have not pure air. The poison of contaminated air finds its way through the lungs into the blood of the animal, and the milk inevitably partakes of the poison. Much of the milk sold in New York is of this poisonous character. For illustration, I would refer to "an inspector's report of the cow stable nuisance," as given to the public through the daily papers by our new Health Board. The stables referred to were devoid of light, ventilation and sewerage, being overcrowded and overheated, with filthy, disgusting stalls, and a filthy condition of the animals themselves. The yard, says the report, was filthy and wet, made so by the manure, urine, and water, which emitted a vile odor. These offensive matters flowed through a ditch into a "good-sized stagnant pond," which occupied the ground, constituting a "decided nuisance, pernicious to health and comfort." So says the report.

PALACES AND STABLES IN NEW YORK CITY—A WORD ABOUT "FRESH MILK"—PEEVISH MOTHERS.

We copy the following article, under the above title, from Dr. Morris Mattson's "Facts for the People," etc., from which we have previously quoted upon the subject of foul or noxious air.

"New York City being the great commercial emporium of the United States," says Dr. Mattson, "we have a great deal of wealth, with all of the refinement and luxury which usually accompanies it, and particularly very splendid up-town residences, which are sometimes designated *palaces*. This is all very well, but when it is found that those palaces are frequently in close connection with *horse and cow stables*, one begins to lose his relish for what may be considered the fascinations and charms of fashionable life. If, indeed, one is a lover of pure air, one would be more likely to sigh for a cottage upon the hillside than a palace in the city.

"But our chief business, in this article, is to speak of a certain up-town palace, owned by a wealthy gentleman, who was the owner also of four or five splendid horses, costing him five or six thousand dollars apiece, and an equally splendid cow, which he had selected from the finest breeds, and for which he paid an exorbitant price. The horses were to gratify his own taste, the cow to gratify the taste of his wife, who had frequently told him that there was nothing so desirable as '*fresh milk*' for the coffee, and fresh milk also for the children. She had heard about slop-fed cows, and had no notion of using milk which came from such questionable sources; she wanted pure, fresh milk from a cow of her own.

"This all looked very reasonable in theory, and the indulgent husband, having purchased the animals in question, was obliged to have a stable for their accommodation. But where to locate it was a difficult question to answer. He knew it was fashionable for New York millionaires to have stables adjacent to their houses, and he had no objection to being in the fashion in this particular, but, unfortunately, he had no spare ground upon which to erect a stable. After due consideration, there seemed to be but one alternative, which was that of placing the stable *under ground;* and one of his poetical neighbors assured him that this was a 'brilliant conception,' inasmuch as the stable would be *out of sight*, and *out of the way*. The thought was not entertained for a moment that cows and horses need an abundance of fresh air, and that this fresh air, with its vitalizing oxygen, is quite as important to them as their daily food and drink.

"The stable was finally completed, under the superintendence of a noted architect, who had it furnished with a number of 'ventilating flues,' which, however, in accordance with one of Dr. Franklin's notions, seemed more inclined to '*draw downward*' than *upward*. In due time the cow and the horses were installed in their new quarters; but scarcely a week had elapsed when it was discovered that the stable was emitting a most disagreeable odor. The 'ventilating flues' did not seem to be rendering much service. It happened about this time that the gentleman of the palace was taking a walk before sunrise, scenting the keen, pure air of the morning; and upon his return, he very naturally opened the stable door to look in upon his splendid cow and favorite horses; but, alas! his unwilling nostrils were saluted by such a perfume from the inclosure, as to render him quite uncertain as to whether he would require any breakfast, and he was not at all sure that the '*fresh milk*' from the cow, of which his wife had said so much, would be particularly agreeable in his coffee.

"Time passed on, and the cow began to droop and sicken; the horses also looked dull, weary, and jaded, with all of the signs of disease, and it was deemed expedient to consult a veterinary surgeon in regard to their health. All this time the poor animals were sickening because they had not enough of pure air to breathe, the atmosphere within the stable being too horrible for description. Escaping from the inclosure, it permeated the house, and was enough to sicken the whole family. Meanwhile, the milk of the cow was still used for family purposes, was given to the children, was put into the tea and coffee, and all without a suspicion that the milk was literally a poison. A cow can not yield pure milk unless she has pure air to breathe; shut her up in a close stable, so that the air about her will soon become contaminated by the poisonous carbonic acid gas from her lungs, and the foul emanations from her body, and she will soon show unmistakable signs of disease. Her milk, in the mean time, will partake of the disease of her body; indeed, it would seem as though the udder of the poor sick cow was a sort of *drainage* whereby nature sought to relieve her general system of some of its impurities. These impurities become incorporated with the milk, which is unfit to be taken into the human stomach. Every intelligent mother knows that her milk is influenced by the condition of her system. If she is peevish and fretful, (from well-assigned causes, perhaps,) her nursing child will be peevish and fretful; if she partakes of food which deranges her digestive organs, her child will be sure, almost, to suffer similar derangements; if she swallows a cathartic, the cathartic effect of the drug will be manifest in the child.

SUB-CELLARS, BASEMENTS, ETC.—GOODS SAVED FROM
RUSTING.

Cellars, basements, etc., may be supplied with a pure air
by my process of ventilation, so as to be fit places of abode,
or suitable for the storage of goods which otherwise might be
injured by the dampness. Attention to this matter would
be the means, oftentimes, of saving thousands of dollars to
the merchant, by the preservation of his goods, to say
nothing of the preservatton of the health and lives of the
occupants of those places.

There was a basement some years ago, in Cortlandt St.,
adjoining the Western Hotel, devoted to the sale of
"Yankee Notions," in which were included many articles
of hardware, which, owing to dampness, rusted badly, so
that a large amount of property was destroyed, or rendered
unsaleable. In addition to this, a very useful employee of
the establishment was constantly indisposed, and finally
left his situation, believing that the place was unhealthy.
Under these circumstances I was employed to ventilate the
place ; and after my task was accomplished, there was no
more rusting of the goods, and the sick employee returned
to his post without making further complaints of ill health.

SHOW-WINDOW VENTILATION.

In many cases this is exceedingly important. With
proper ventilation the moisture is prevented from accumulating upon the glass, which freezes when the weather is
sufficiently cold, and renders the glass impervious to the
sight. Besides, the freezing is liable to fracture the glass,
which is usually quite expensive. A pane of glass in one
of the show-windows of the late International Hotel, New
York City, was fractured in this way, and could not be
replaced short of several hundred dollars.

My mode of ventilating a show-window is different from
that employed in any other kind of ventilation, although
the principle is obviously the same. The store connected
with the window may, if desired, be ventilated, as well as

the window itself, and a pure air furnished to the whole of the connecting apartments.

A show-window not ventilated is a hot, dry place in summer, and goods displayed in it are frequently injured, or rendered unsaleable. Straw goods are liable to be injured, and silks and ribbons have their colors changed. Meat and poultry hung up in windows for display are in much danger of spoiling. The very choicest goods which a store can produce are generally placed in the show-windows; and it is desirable that they should be preserved from change or injury. This may be accomplished by my system of ventilation, which has been successfully adopted.

WASHINGTON CITY POST OFFICE—A FACT FOR THE SKEPTICAL —ORDERS FROM JAY COOKE AND GEORGE W. RIGGS, THE NOTED BANKERS.

Post offices, like banking houses, need ventilation now and then. The mail-bags and leather pouches, when exposed to a damp atmosphere, are liable to become mouldy, and the atmosphere itself is very objectionable to those who have any regard for their health. All that is here said will apply to the post office in Washington City, which I had the pleasure of ventilating, and I can not well refrain from appending the following letter by the Hon. S. J. Bowen, the postmaster. The letter was written to a gentleman in New York City, without a suspicion, so far as I know, that it would come under my observation:

WASHINGTON, December 20, 1865.

MR. GAY: There has been in operation in the post office in this city one of Gouge's Ventilators for the past two months. It was put in for the purpose of ventilating the basement, in which are stored the mail-bags and pouches from which a supply for other offices is drawn.

Before the Ventilator was put up, the air in the room was damp and impure, so much so as to be very disagreeable and unhealthy to persons remaining in it any length of time; and the leather pouches would be covered with mould and the sacks and bags with mildew. The Ventilator has removed both the bad air and the dampness, and a person can discover no difference in the air from that in the rooms above. The pouches and bags are now perfectly dry, and we think the Ventilator has already saved to the Department double its cost in preventing injury to them.

It was put up as an experiment, to be paid for if it succeeded. We would not have it removed for any consideration whatever. I think it will be very generally adopted in this city.

Truly yours, etc.,

S. J. BOWEN, *Postmaster.*

The experiment of ventilating the Washington post office having been entirely successful, it attracted the attention of Jay Cooke and George W. Riggs, the noted bankers, who were so much pleased with what had been done, that each one complimented me with an order to ventilate his banking-house in Washington City.

BANK-VAULTS.

These are not unfrequently pervaded by a damp atmosphere, which causes books, papers, and documents to become mouldy. Proper ventilation will render the air pure and dry, so that there will be no tendency of the books and papers to mould.

POWDER-MAGAZINES.

These magazines, I am informed, are very liable to become damp, which injures the powder, destroying its granular condition, and causing it to form in concrete masses. An ordnance officer at the Brooklyn Navy Yard, who had acquired some knowledge of my system of ventilation, suggested to me that it would be likely to prove valuable in connection with powder-magazines, and confirmed what is mentioned above in relation to the powder. He felt persuaded that my *Atmospheric Ventilator* would obviate every difficulty, and save much money to the Government and others who deal in the article. He spoke in commendation of another feature of the apparatus, which, no doubt, would be a desideratum, namely, the safe and efficient light which it would afford to the interior of the magazine. This light, it may be added, would be free from all danger of causing an explosion of the powder.

SAILING VESSELS, ETC.—COMMODORE FOOTE.

My method of ventilation can be applied to sailing vessels, steamboats, emigrant ships, etc., as easily and successfully as to school-rooms, churches, kitchens, sleeping-rooms, or parlors ; and yet I have never had an opportunity of ventilating a sea-going vessel. I was applied to by Commodore Foote, just previous to his death, to examine the receiving-ship North Carolina, lying at our navy-yard, which he was very anxious to have ventilated; but the matter was referred to the authorities at Washington, and before it was decided, the death of Commodore Foote took place at the Astor House. Since then there has been no action in the matter. I hope I may yet have an opportunity of rendering my services in this species of ventilation.

An old sea-captain tells me that the hold of a ship, in which the cargo is principally stored, is sure to become very damp if ventilation is not resorted to, and a copious condensation of moisture will take place on the under surface of the deck and the sides of the vessel. The water thus condensed will fall from the deck upon the cargo, and injure or destroy all perishable goods, as silks, cloths, sugars, teas, etc. As efficient ventilation would prevent the difficulties here spoken of, merchants and shippers might save themselves from heavy losses without much expenditure of money. Ventilation would also preserve the timbers of a ship, which are rotted by foul air. Ships, it would seem, are sometimes completely rotted by foul air within the short period of three years. It would certainly be economy for every ship-owner to incur a slight expense in ventilating his ship, rather than to take the chance of its total destruction.

VENTILATION—PURE AIR—HEALTH.

The subject matter under this head has been used as a *special circular*, and is reproduced here because many of the paragraphs, as originally intended, will serve as brief or partial answers to questions which are frequently put to us in reference to the feasibility of ventilating particular places or buildings which have become injurious to health, or, to say the least, offensive to the sense of smell.

PARLORS.—"Can my parlor be ventilated?" is a common question. The answer is, "Yes." Moreover, parlors should always have a pure atmosphere. Social pleasures are exceedingly marred by a pent-up or foul atmosphere. Pure air will give a finer sparkle to wit, merriment and repartee, than the choicest brands of Champagne. Let it be remembered, also, that gas-lights, in proportion to their number and brilliancy, will render the air impure and unfit to be taken into the lungs, unless there is adequate ventilation. Five cubic feet of carbonic acid, we are told, is formed by the burning of an ordinary gas jet an hour, consuming in the meantime five cubic feet of gas. Multiply these five feet of carbonic acid with the number of gas jets, and it will readily be perceived what an atmosphere of poisonous carbonic acid is floating in one's parlor, to say nothing of the carbonic acid which is constantly evolved from the lungs of the occupants.

SLEEPING ROOMS.—No higher boon could be conferred upon the human family than to supply them with a perfectly pure air during the night, while asleep. It would impart new vigor to the life forces, and add immeasurably to the health. Invalids and children particularly require this pure air during the night while asleep.

KITCHENS.—The foul air of kitchens is one of the greatest discomforts of domestic life. The kitchen odor not only diffuses itself through the whole house, but attaches itself to the garments of the domestics, and of every one who much frequents the kitchen, and renders them more or less offensive when they come into one's presence. Kitchens properly ventilated will always have a pure and sweet atmosphere.

CELLARS.—The damp, foul air of a cellar, contaminating more or less the atmosphere of one's house, is a prolific source of disease, though frequently not suspected. It may always be remedied by ventilation.

WATER CLOSETS.—Those "modern improvements," however necessary to our wants, are frequently great nuisances, and oftentimes seriously affect the health. They may be rendered perfectly sweet by ventilation.

CHURCHES.—It is not dull sermons which cause people to go to sleep in churches half so frequently as the impure atmosphere. How can people keep awake in an atmosphere loaded with carbonic acid, and other poisons emanating from the human body, which they are obliged to breathe constantly for two hours or more. The atmosphere of a crowded church is closely analagous to that of a room in which charcoal is permitted to burn, without any admission of fresh air.

LEGISLATIVE HALLS.—If our Legislative Halls were better ventilated, we should have better legislative enactments, better laws, and a higher regard for the public welfare. Bad air produces bad blood, gives rise to a fierce or petulent temper, and creates an inordinate desire, in many instances, for tobacco, ardent spirits, opium, and other body and soul-destroying agencies. The foul air of our Legislative Halls, Churches, and other public buildings in which human beings are densely crowded together, is a disgrace to our age and civilization

POOR HOUSES.—One can not bestow upon the poor a more valuable gift than that of pure air. They should be provided with this, to say the least, though they may have no other comfort.

PROVISION CLOSETS.—Food is frequently distasteful, as well as injurious to health, in consequence of its absorption of noxious gases in refrigerators and provision closets. It is frequently claimed that refrigerators are ventilated, but it is not so—at least, the ventilation is very imperfect. Butter, milk, meat, bread, vegetables, fruit, and everything we eat, should be kept in a pure atmosphere, or they will be more or less tainted, and rendered unfit for food.

HORSE STABLES.—Have mercy on your horses. Never allow a valuable horse to become blind for the want of pure air. Remember that a stable can not be efficiently ventilated by flues.

SHIPS AND STEAMERS.—Commerce is the golden link by which nationalities are bound together, and yet we should not forget that it was through our commerce that the Asiatic cholera—that terrible scourge—was brought repeatedly to our shores. Let us hold on to our commerce, but get rid of the evils with which it is connected. Avaricious ship-owners have crowded human beings so closely together in their ships, that the foul air, thus generated, was more than sufficient to produce or keep alive the pestilence. Had all ships coming to our shores been properly ventilated, we should have had no cholera. Had ship-owners expended a little money in adequate ventilation, it would have saved thousands of precious lives, and the expenditure of vast sums of treasure. It is well known that some of the steamers arriving in New York from Europe had *cholera* in the steerage, where the air was foul, while there was none of it in the closely adjacent cabin, where the air was comparatively pure. *Foul air* and *cholera* are synonomous terms. Let the bitter experience of the *past* teach us a salutary lesson for the *future*.

SCHOOL-HOUSE VENTILATION. — Notwithstanding the teachings of Chemistry and Physiology, it does not yet seem to be understood in our schools that carbonic acid is a poor substitute for oxygen, in the breathing process; that fresh air is indispensable to health; that the pent-up, stifling air of our school-rooms sadly deteriorates the health of both pupil and teacher, rendering the brain torpid or inactive, and interfering more or less with study and mental development. It is a mournful fact that many of our brightest and most hopeful children die while getting their education, and it has not yet been estimated how many of them die from the confined and poisonous air of the school-room, superadded to excessive study and over-tasked brains. In our treatise on ventilation, which we offer to the public gratuitously, we have quoted a distinguished member of the Board of Education in New York City, Mr. Hayes, as saying that the teachers of our schools usually die of consumption in six or seven years. This fact should deeply impress every one who has any interest in the subject of education.

SECRET OF VENTILATION.—Millions of money have been expended in the United States and Europe in reference to different plans of ventilation, but never with satisfactory results, because the inventors have not availed themselves of an adequate *motive power*. Air can not be moved without an adequate force any more than a cannon ball, and therefore it is impossible to get *foul air* out of a building, or *fresh air* into it, without a motive power which is equal to the emergency. This motive power, consisting of a rapid, up-moving current of air, is furnished by "Gouge's Atmospheric Ventilator," and when properly adapted to the building, or place to be ventilated, will never fail in producing the most satisfactory results.

DICKENS ON VENTILATION.

[The following remarks on ventilation, by Mr. Charles Dickens, are now published with his name for the first time. We are indebted for this privilege to Mr. Stephen English, editor of the *Insurance Times*, a valuable monthly periodical, published in this city, and circulating largely in Europe. Mr. English was the intimate friend of Mr. Dickens in England, while the latter was a reporter, and when he visited this city in the capacity of a public reader, Mr. English besought him to write an article for his journal upon ventilation. Mr. Dickens at first refused, saying that his visit to America was not for the purpose of using his pen; but, upon further importunity, he consented to oblige his old friend, provided he would not announce his name as the author. Under these restrictions, the article was published in the *Insurance Times*, in August, 1869; and, now that Mr. Dickens has gone to his long home, Mr. English considers that there is no impropriety in disclosing the authorship, He has, therefore, freely permitted us to make use of the article.

Mr. Dickens, it would seem, was employed in a drug store in London before he became a reporter, and it was in that capacity, perhaps, that his intuitive and comprehensive mind enabled him to unravel something of the mysteries of the circulation of the blood, and to assure himself that we can neither have good blood nor good health, unless we have pure air to breathe. Though Dickens is dead, his utilitarian spirit will long survive.]

There are few principles of health better understood than ventilation. There is probably none more disregarded. Pure air is essential to health, because essential to purify the blood. Good blood is good health; and in a large degree good air is good blood. This is an old and obvious truth, but ignored almost universally.

Let us look into this matter a little. Insurance men are interested in it, because their offices are as a general thing illy constructed as regards ventilation, and almost always destructive of health. They are convenient; they are fitted up with a view to facilitating business, and that

is all. Business was the idea. Health was not thought of ;
ventilation, if mentioned, was set aside as a whim of dreaming enthusiasts who would like to become philosophers.
But there are some facts about the subject. If anything is
understood by our physiologists, it is the relation of air to
blood and of blood to health.

Thus it is known that the heart is a double organ. There
is a *right* side and there is a *left* side, and the functions of
these two sides or parts are entirely distinct and unlike.
But a primal and all important office of the heart is to *force
the blood to the lungs for ventilation*. As the blood is
received into the heart from the veins, it is laden with foul
matter, waste material of the system which it has gathered
in its journey around the body. It is not red, but dark and
impure. These impurities are thrown out largely by means
of expiration, and hence we avoid air that has been once
breathed. It contains a deadly poison, carbonic acid, in
which, if a lighted candle is placed, it is immediately extinguished. The "Black Hole of Calcutta" derives its name
from the fact that about one hundred and fifty foreigners
were confined there with little or no ventilation. When
the dungeon was opened ten hours later, one hundred and
twenty-three were dead ! They had died from breathing
their own breaths that contained carbonic acid and animal
matter from their own bodies.

We say that one of the cardinal functions of the heart
is to send the blood to the lungs for ventilation. In doing
this the labor of the two parts of the heart may be clearly seen
and distinguished. Thus, it is the *right* side or part of the
heart that sends the impure blood up to the lungs for purification. It goes through what is called the *pulmonary
artery* into the air-cells and minute blood vessels (capillaries) of the lungs, and *while there* is entirely changed in
its character. The oxygen which we have breathed from
the air rushes through the thin coats of the air-cells and
capillaries, and unites with the blood ; and at the same
time the carbonic acid rushes out from the blood through
the same thin coats, and is ejected by expiration. In this
manner the color of the blood is changed to bright red, and
the impurities disappear. It is fitted for its life-giving
work. When this is accomplished, and it is prepared for

its office in the body, it is sent back to the *left side* or part of the heart through the pulmonary veins. The *left* side then performs its duty, which is to send the *pure* blood to every part of the system through the arteries.

It will be observed that the *right* side of the heart sends *impure* blood to the lungs for purification, while the *left* side sends *pure* blood to all parts of the body. Pure blood thus dispatched to the extremities of the body returns through the veins again laden with impurities to the *right* side of the heart, which again sends it to the lungs for ventilation as before.

When it is remembered that it is the blood that forms our bones, flesh, and even the hairs of our head, it will not appear strange that nature struggles to keep the blood pure, and that the heart toils and throbs to send it out to the air. It never ceases its efforts for ventilation till it ceases to beat, or until we have ceased to live.

But we often abuse the heart by responding to its call for ventilation with fetid, impure air, which instead of purifying the blood adds to the poison already within it. The heart calls for bread and we give it a stone, for a fish, and we give it a serpent! Impure air frustrates the purposes of nature, and to a great extent neutralizes its efforts to preserve the body in health. Manifestly if the blood is impure which builds the body, the body will not be sound. Good morals are not made of bad actions, and good bread is not made of bad wheat. We cannot, therefore, expect health when the vital elements that make it are wanting.

There is, then, a direct relation between air and blood, between blood and life. All animal life calls for air. The trees and plants and flowers unite in the call, and die when their plea is unanswered. To deny ourselves pure air, is to express contempt for the mechanism of our being, and to invite the vengeance of disease and death. It mocks the throbbing heart, it derides the lungs, and scorns the stream which carries our life.

Ventilation is an important principle of health. It is important that clerks and employees avoid those offices that are low, damp, dark, or badly constructed in respect to air. The pale, white cheek is not the healthy one, but it tells of confinement in badly ventilated rooms. It tells of blood but partially purified in the lungs, and of vital elements gone, of waste matter that will finally take the form of tubercles, and end in consumption and death.

There is moral wrong in constructing badly ventilated rooms, and there is moral wrong in abiding in them when they are constructed. To hire men to labor in them is but buying for money their health, their happiness and their life. And for men to accept such positions there is no adequate excuse: they are purchasing death.

DOUBLE windows and heavy panes of glass, with a view to saving heat, are well advised, but they should be used in connection with ventilation. If the windows fit so tightly as to exclude the outer air, and there is no other channel for its admission, the arrangement will be dangerous to health and life. A house in which warmth and ventilation are not twin-sisters is unfit for a human habitation. We knew a millionaire who had his house fitted with double windows, and his doors plied with weather-strips, but there was no ventilation, which he considered a delusion. He became an invalid in less than a month, and in less than three months he was dead.

ARM-CHAIR GLEANINGS AND JOTTINGS.

Under this title, with scissors and paste within our reach, we propose to exercise a sort of editorial function, and to weave into our editorial web many fragments which are too valuable to be lost. In our web, therefore, each of these fragments will have a conspicuous place and a conspicuous heading, standing out in bold relief, analagous to the figures of an embroidered garment. Since the publication of the first edition of our book on ventilation in 1866, the subject seems to have excited very great attention. It is not unusual now to find articles upon ventilation in the newspapers and magazines, with discussions in reference to the dangerous effects of foul air in our schools, dwellings, and various public places. Editors, judges, clergymen, and literary celebrities have been participating in the discussion with an earnestness which shows how deeply they are interested in the theme. Those "driftings of the public mind" have not been overlooked in our arm-chair gleanings, and we take pleasure in presenting them to the notice and consideration of our readers.

THE AIR WE BREATHE—HORRIBLE FACTS.—We clip the following from a newspaper whose title we are unable to give, but we have noticed similar articles in the scientific and medical journals, and have no doubt of the truth and accuracy of the facts presented:

"A scientific Parisian has had the curiosity to make an analysis of the air that is breathed in a theatre, or any close audience-room that contains a great number of persons, with the following horrible results : He carried into a theatre at ten o'clock at night a bottle of ice placed on a plate, and then collected the vapor which rapidly condensed on the outside of the bottle and flowed down on to the plate. At first, the vapor thus collected had the smell, the taste, and, so far as could be determined, every chemical quality belonging to the waters of the most deadly fever marshes Under the microscope, this water was at first clear, but soon, that is to say in a week, it was found to be full of fine animalculæ. A little later on, these animalculæ had grown, and the big ones were seen pursuing and devouring the little ones. Still later on, at the end of two months, the water was thick with animalculæ, various forms were seen, and still the work of destruction was going on. At last, but three hideous monsters were seen—microscopic monsters, of course, since they were contained in a drop of water—and these were still fighting to see which could devour the other. At the end of three months, the water became transparent."

A FATAL WARNING.—The annexed article is from the *New York Tribune* of May 11, 1867, and may therefore be considered authentic. The article should be carefully read and deeply pondered, as it is one of the many proofs of the danger we are in from foul air, without seeming to be conscious of the fact:

"The Moravian Seminary at Bethlehem, Pa., has long been widely popular as a high school for young ladies. Its trustees and principal are probably as competent and faithful as those of almost any similar academy. Yet it seems that they have but one bedroom, twenty-five by twelve feet, for their *eight* servant-girls, and that this room, on the basement floor adjoining the kitchen, had but a single window and a door ; and that, these being closed, (as, of course, they usually were while the girls slept,) there was absolutely no ventilation and no admission of fresh air! True, there was a single flue, which led from this room up into the pupils' dining-room overhead ; but this flue was generally shut up, or only opened through a stove-pipe which led into the chimney. The stove being taken down on the return of spring, the pipe was allowed to remain, and down this pipe the gas from the stove above was regularly driven, filling the girls' bedroom with its poisonous fumes, until, on Sunday night last, it killed two of them outright and probably will kill one more. Of the remainder, two were badly and two more but slightly injured. The eighth did not retire till toward morning, when she discovered the mischief, though she did not comprehend it till daylight.

" Of course, this is not murder, but ignorance—gross, shameful, guilty ignorance. No person has any right to undertake the most responsible charge of a seminary who does not know that a close bedroom is perilous to the health and life of even *one* human being, and more than eight times as perilous when its inmates are increased to eight. Had the managers of the Moravian Seminary known what it was their duty to know, and had they nevertheless packed these eight girls into one unventilated room, they *would* have been murderers of the darkest dye. Their ignorance palliates, but does not excuse, their wrong-doing. What will palliate the crime of the next set of wholesale homicides by means of unventilated bedrooms, or class-rooms, or halls for public meetings ?"

"POPULAR SUFFOCATION."—The *New York World* of recent date, under the foregoing significant caption, has a scathing article in relation to the pestiferous atmospheres to be found in our theatres and public places of resort. The editor applies his caustic without stint or mercy, and we trust that his *editorial surgery* will be followed by good results   Violent diseases, the doctors say, require violent remedies.

From the report of Dr. R. C. Stiles to the Board of Health, we learn that the inmates of our theatres breathe a vitiated atmosphere, in which the proportion of carbonic acid gas ranges as high as seven parts in a thousand, which, when we consider that two parts in a thousand is the limit of healthful endurance, is not apt to stimulate agreeable reflections in the minds of the valetudinarians who desire to patronize these places. What with the respiration of hundreds of people, and the combustion of hundreds of gas-jets—any one of which latter, Dr. Stiles pleasantly informs us, consumes as much oxygen as five persons—the interior of our places of recreation are converted into houses of popular suffocation. Dr. Stiles, it must be understood, made his tests only in the larger and more fashionable resorts, where many expedients have been employed to obtain pure air. What his report would be like were he to visit some of the no less popular but less fashionable resorts, it would be difficult to say. There are several places on Broadway, and one or two on the Bowery, where the crowded audiences fester night after night in their own exhalations; where the miasms are dense enough to dim the lights in the upper parts of the house, and the foul and deadly atmosphere is breathed over and over by sweltering people, while its humidity condenses on the dirty walls, and trickles like a death-sweat all round the poisonous auditorium. If the gutters and courts of the lower wards need chloride of lime occasionally, surely these pestiferous places need ventilation.

"THE HOUSE WE LIVE IN."—This phrase originated with the late Dr. William Alcott, and was the title of one of his excellent books on Health. The "House We Live In" he described as our physical organization, consisting of bones, muscles, nerves, etc. This is important, and should receive due attention ; but it is equally important to keep in view the house or dwelling in which the physical body is lodged or accommodated. It is here that we are born, here that we live, here that we die, but unfortunately we often die prematurely. This brings us to the study of ventilation, for foul air is more frequently the cause of premature deaths than anything else. If the reader should be in doubt on this subject, let him refer to our chapter on Zymotic Diseases, page 11. He will there see that half of the deaths in New York City and Brooklyn, during the hot summer months, are caused by the zymotic or foul-air diseases. This is frightful, and should cause the people to wake up to a true sense of their danger. An individual may inhale enough of atmospheric poison in a single hour to bring on a tedious sickness, or perhaps destroy life. The abiding place of the physical body, therefore, should receive careful attention. The merchant in his counting-room, the clergyman in his study, the lawyer in his office, the artist in his studio, the mechanic in his workshop, the housewife in her parlor or kitchen, and above all, children and young people in their schools or seminaries, should each and all be abundantly supplied with pure air during the busy hours of the day. This will improve the health and physical condition, and increase the activity of the mental powers. Labors which are heavy or oppressive, will become comparatively light and easy. The burdens of life, which are scarcely thought of while the system is in its ordinary healthful and elastic condition, become a camel's load under the depressing influence of foul air. . . . Passing from the busy day to the quiet and solitary night, we should be especially careful to have a pure air to breathe while we are asleep, for it is then that Nature seeks to build up and restore the exhausted system. If we fail in this, we are likely to get up in the morning with a feeling of languor or weariness, having no relish for food, and no inclination to enter upon the duties or responsibilities of the day. The remedy for all this is pure air, which can be only obtained through efficient ventilation. Obey the scriptural injunction, "Set thy house in order." If man is to be eaten by worms, as Kate Field says in her Adirondack story of the deer-shooting, there is no good reason why he should become a feast for worms in advance of his time.

BENJAMIN FRANKLIN — EVERY CREVICE CLOSED — WEATHER-STRIPS. — This distinguished philosopher, who had so keen an insight into the physical forces of nature and the physical things of life, said, nearly a century ago, "Some are as much afraid of fresh air as persons with hydrophobia are of fresh water. I myself had formerly this prejudice—this *œrophobia*, as I now account it—and dreading the supposed dangerous effects of cool air, I considered it an enemy, and closed, with extreme care, every crevice in the rooms I inhabited. Experience has convinced me of my error. I now look upon fresh air as a friend ; I even sleep with an open window. I am persuaded that no common air from without is so unwholesome as the air within a close room that has been often breathed and not changed. . . . Physicians have of late happily discovered, after a contrary opinion for some ages that fresh and cool air does good to persons with small-pox, and various fevers. It is to be hoped that in another century or two, we shall all find out that it is not bad even for people in health."

With regard to draughts of air, of which people seem to be so much afraid, it may be stated that such draughts are chiefly injurious when they strike upon the back of the neck ; they do not seem to be injurious when they come directly into the face. These suggestions of Franklin, in relation to draughts of air, and the dangerous habit of closing every crevice in one's apartments, must be prejudicial to the *Weather-Strip* business. A friend at our elbow thinks that weather-strips are the nails of our premature coffins.

FILTHY CELLARS IN FIRST-CLASS HOUSES. — It is not only in tenement-houses that we have filthy cellars and apartments, but also in our "brown-stone fronts," claiming to be first-class houses. During the memorable summer of 1866, the well-known Dr. Dalton reported to the Board of Health that in many of the best private houses in our city the cellars were surcharged with rubbish of various sorts, which rendered them detrimental to the health of the residents, as well as to the entire neighborhood in which they were located. He urged whitewashing as a disinfecting and cleansing process. If our rich people would give a little more attention than they do to whitewashing and ventilation, they would have less sickness and fewer premature deaths in their elegant houses than at present.

Dr. WILLARD PARKER AND THE CHOLERA.—It would seem, so far as the fatality of cholera is concerned, that it makes a great difference whether the individual suffering with it is shut up in a house, or is out of doors, exposed to the open air. Dr. Parker has given us some valuable information on this point. Addressing himself to the Board of Health, during the summer of 1866, he said, "Ship fever and cholera are very similar in their mode of propagation. I remember when Bellevue Hospital was crowded with this disease. The beds were full, the floors were covered, and when we went into the building in the morning, we could not get along without stepping over dead bodies. When we could do nothing else, we concluded to put up some tents in the open air, and let the poor fellows take their chances there. *Every one of them recovered.* In another instance, a ship drifted ashore in the North River, with eighty-four cases on board. *They were taken out upon the bank, and they recovered.*"

Can we have any better evidence than this of the virulence of stagnant air as it frequently exists in unventilated houses? And yet it is only here and there that we find an individual who deems it important to have his house or place of business ventilated.

POISONED AIR.—Dr. Lemuel Dickinson, of Colchester, Connecticut, who died in 1868, attributed his sickness to breathing the poisoned air of a dissecting-room. He said he felt the foul air penetrate to his lungs, and this peculiar sensation he could never remove. The *Philadelphia Ledger* is authority for the above statement.

AIR OF HOSPITALS. — Mr. Lund, of Manchester, in a paper read before the British Medical Association, and reported in the London *Lancet* of August 15, 1868, detailed some experiments which he had made on the air in one of the surgical wards of the Manchester Royal Infirmary. The ward in which the experiments were conducted contained four beds, and had a cubical capacity of about 5,400 feet. A fluid ounce of distilled water was placed in a pint stoppered glass bottle, and by removing the stopper, raising the bottle sharply through the air, reclosing and quickly shaking it, the water and the air were intimately mixed ; and this process was repeated in all fully five hundred times, until the water, previously transparent, had become slightly opalescent. In the deposit thus thrown down, after forty-eight hours, distinct evidence of the presence of organic life was perceptible under the microscope, and on the fifth day there were numerous actively moving vorticelli, with abundance of monads in ceaseless motion. Thus, it was inferred that the presence in the air of microscopic organic germs was a constant condition easily detectable.

If these microscopic germs are peculiar to the atmosphere of hospitals, the sooner hospitals are ventilated the better it will be for the patients and other inmates These germs, according to medical authority, may have much to do in producing hospital gangrene, erysipelas, and kindred diseases.

THE BLACK-HOLE OF CALCUTTA.—This historic Black-Hole is now frequently spoken of in connection with ventilation. Its exact whereabouts has not been distinctly settled, but the place itself is described as being something less than twenty feet square. Within this enclosure, on a night in June, 1756, one hundred and forty-six men were confined, and only twenty-three of them came out alive on the following morning. The old fort of Calcutta has been pulled down, and it is stated that Dr. Norman Chevers, a writer on sanitary matters, had his attention drawn to a room or enclosure which is described as "the exact counterpart of the Black-Hole."

IRISH STEAMER LONDONDERRY.—This steamer is closely akin to the Black-Hole. On the night of December 1, 1848, it was threatened by a storm. The captain drove one hundred and fifty of the deck passengers into a small cabin, and closed the hatches upon them. In the morning, seventy of these were found suffocated.

WHAT HUMBOLDT SAYS.— "Could the atmosphere we breathe, even in our dwellings, be rendered pure and healthful, how much more of life could we enjoy, and how much more could be accomplished that we undertake Our plans would not be so often interrupted by disease, nor would the work commenced by us be left undone in consequence of premature death."

AIR FROM A GREAT HEIGHT.—The crotchet in ventilation of taking air from a great height seems to be losing its advocates. In ventilating the House of Commons, which required 2,500,000 cubic feet of air per hour, the original plan of getting the supply of air from the clock-tower was given up, because it was found that the atmosphere of London, at that altitude, was not as pure as that nearer the earth. The supply is now drawn from the Star Court and the Commons Court. So far as the carbonic acid of the atmosphere is concerned, we do not get rid of it by ascending to a great height, as proved by the authority of De Saussure, and other distinguished observers. (See page 136)

SUSAN B. ANTHONY.—This noted lady has some sensible ideas in relation to pure air, whatever may be said of her political teachings. In the *Revolution* she pointed out the impurity of the air of our public schools, and said that if the Board of Education had to trundle all the air consumed in our schools in wheelbarrows from a distance, there would be some excuse for their negligence in providing pure air.

THE WORST POISON!—WHERE DOES IT COME FROM? —This question is answered by the *New York Times* in the following caustic but sensible remarks:

People are just now talking of precautions against poison. The worst poison does not come from the druggists. It comes from our modes of ventilation, or rather of non-ventilation; and our practice in this respect is a satire on our pretensions to science. Our city reading-rooms and libraries are almost all badly ventilated. In summer the side-windows of the apartments are opened, and the *thorough-draught*, which, at times, is strong enough to flutter the leaves of the books, "fills one's bones with aitches" and shortens the lives of literary invalids. In winter the burnt-out heavy air of stoves, or other heaters, is equally murderous; for then doors and windows are shut, and none but the youngest and most robust can pass an hour in such atmospheres without asphyxia, or something very near it. 'Tis dreadful to see and feel such things in the very seats of intellect and science. Poison! Our deadliest poison goes into the lungs and not into the stomach.

THADDEUS STEVENS.—Great men as well as little men die for the want of pure air. Mr. Stevens, mentioned above, was a distinguished lawyer, legislator, and statesman, with a vast and comprehensive intellect; but with all of his erudition and stores of knowledge, he seems not to have learned that pure air was one of the grand requisites of health. He was specially the victim of foul air. While in Washington, his time was divided between the Capitol and his private residence. The Capitol is proverbial for its foul air, while his residence, in which he sought to "renew his strength," was a small, dilapidated building, in which fresh air could not have been an abundant commodity. Here is a description, by a Washington letter-writer, of the house in which Mr. Stevens lived and died ; and we are not sure but that it might prove an acceptable contribution to our literature, so far as architecture is concerned, if we could have a full description of the houses in which all of our eminent men have lived and died :

I found Mr. Stevens in a small, shabby, low-roofed room of a small, dilapidated brick house in a not very pleasant-looking and certainly an unfrequented street. He had evidently chosen it for convenience rather than comfort or style. A very plain, low-posted bedstead, a small wardrobe and bureau, a desk and an easy-chair formed the furniture of the room. The decorations consisted only of photographs of Mr. Lincoln and himself, and one of Miss Vinnie Ream's busts, but whether of Mr. Lincoln or himself I can not now remember. Mr. Stevens was lying on the bed, his head tied up in a red handkerchief, and his feet in a pair of plain slippers ; he was minus coat and vest. So nearly complete was his *dishabille* that he alluded to it on my entry, and said he was compelled to rest all he could, and that when not at the Capitol he was seeking renewed strength in repose. It was not sleep he wanted, only rest for his bones in a reclining attitude, and he was ready and able to talk as long as he had interested hearers.

THE WORLD MOVES.—Here is a paragraph from the *Tribune* of November 30, which may be read with profit by school-committees, and all others who have anything to do with the management of public buildings :

We are extremely glad that the Board of Controllers in Philadelphia have determined to raise the salaries of school teachers ; but one of the reasons assigned in the report of the committee—that "teachers are required to spend six hours per day in an injurious atmosphere"—strikes us as rather melancholy. Is the increase of salary intended benevolently to render it easier for the teacher to discharge doctor's bills? That would be only just; but it would follow, as a logical necessity, that the public should also defray all the medical expenses of pupils poisoned or thrown into an asphyxia, or committed to the tender mercies of typhoid, by the confinement of "six hours per day in an injurious atmosphere." As the Philadelphia Controllers are in a liberal mood, why not make a moderate appropriation for ventilators?

SLEEP.—*Harper's Weekly* is always full of good things. In addition to its illustrations, it contains much valuable reading matter. Below, for example, is an article on "Sleep," which we commend to the reader on account of the remark that the body is more accessible to deleterious influenee at night than by day, and that the air, therefore, ought to be fresh, and the supply plentiful. We may add, that with pure air to breathe during the night, the chances of disease would be very slight. If people could only be impressed with this fact, they would not be long in having their sleeping-rooms ventilated:

Sleep, which is a kind of anticipation of death, is in lifetime a death which restores vitality. It procures the happiness of being born again every day. The better the sleep, the greater the probability of longevity. Night ought to be consecrated to sleep. This is a law of nature which can not be infringed with impunity. Nothing is more prejudicial to longevity than devoting the nights to intellectual or bodily labors. Many literary men, learned men, and artists, have died young in consequence of this practice. On the other hand, early rising, after being refreshed by sleep, is as beneficial as late work is the reverse. The amonnt of sleep necessary for reinvigoration depends upon the age, habits, and constitution of the individual. A new-born infant would perish if kept awake for twenty four hours. Sleep is even more necessary after mental than after bodily labor. A man who thinks little is always in a kind of torpor. Old age, again, requires less sleep than youth and adult age. As the body is more accessible to deleterious influences at night than by day, the air ought also to be fresh, and the supply plentiful. The stomach should not be loaded. The bed should not be too soft, and, if possible, the head should lie to the north, the feet to the south. The head should never be covered by the clothes; but there should be more outer clothing at night than in the daytime, the temperature of the body not being so high. It is a good thing, on taking off one's day clothes, to lay aside also all thoughts of the past. It is only thus that complete relaxation of the mind, as well as of the body, is secured, and without this unbending of the mental faculties perfect sleep is impossible.

HORACE GREELEY ON FARM LIFE, FRESH AIR, ETC.— All Christendom is acquainted with Horace Greeley as the leading editor and master-spirit of the *New York Tribune*. There is an article by him in the *Tribune* of October 9th, 1868, entitled "Greeley's Recollections of a Busy Life." In this he speaks of his preference for an agricultural life, with its pure air and renovating sunshine ; of the death of four of his children, who would not have died, he thinks, if they had been born and reared in the country ; of the choice of his wife in the selection of a farm; and of the love which he has for the forest, where he can wield the ax unmolested, which, he says, is his doctor as well as delight. We append the article, somewhat abbreviated, as it is closely akin to the subject of ventilation :

I am content with my lot, and grateful for the generosity wherewith my labors have been rewarded; and yet I say that were I now to begin my life anew, I would choose to earn my bread by cultivating the soil. Blessed is he whose day's exertion ends with the evening twilight, and who can sleep unbrokenly and without anxiety till the dawn awakes him, with energies renewed and senses brightened by fresh activity, and that fullness of health and vigor which are vouchsafed to those only who spend most of their waking hours in the free, pure air and renovating sunshine of the open country.

I *would* have been a farmer had any science of farming been known to those among whom my earlier boyhood was passed. . . . I can not remember that I had ever seen a periodical devoted to farming, up to the day wherein, in my sixteenth year, I abandoned the farm for the printery. A book which treated of Agriculture, or seeking to set forth the *rationale* of its processes, the natural laws on which they are based, I certainly had not seen. Nay, more; during the ten or twelve years in which I attended school, more or less, I never saw a treatise on Chemistry, Geology, or Botany, in a school-room. I hardly saw one anywhere. That true Agriculture is a grand, ennobling science, based on other sciences, and its pursuit a liberal, elevating profession, was not even hinted, much less inculcated in any essay, speech, sermon, book, pamphlet, or periodical, so far as I then knew. Farming, as understood and practiced by those among whom I grew up, was a work for oxen; and for me the life of an ox had no charms. Most of those I knew seemed to till the earth mainly because they could not help it; and I felt that *I could* help it. So I shook from my brogans the dust of the potato-patch, and stepped out in quest of employment better suited to an intelligent, moral being.

It was a quarter of a century after this before I felt able to buy or make the farm whereon to abide the coming of decay and death. I had been some twenty years a resident of the city, and fifteen the head of a household. Six children had been born to me, and four of them had died—as I am confident some of them would not so prematurely have done, had they been born and reared in the country.

I had earned and bought a small but satisfactory house in the very heart of the city ; but who, if he has any choice, prefers to grow old and die at No. 239, unknown to and uncared for by the denizens of Nos. 237 and 241 ? For my family's sake, if not for my own, a country home was required, so I looked about and found one.

The choice was substantially directed by my wife, who said she insisted upon but three requisites. 1. A peerless spring of pure, soft, living water. 2. A cascade or brawling brook. 3. Woods largely composed of evergreens. These may seem light matters, yet I was some time in finding them grouped on the same small plat, within reasonable distance from the city.

I *did* find them, however, and those who object to my taste in choosing for my home a rocky, wooded, hillside, sloping to the north of west, with a bog at its foot, can not judge me fairly unless they consider the above requirements.

The woods are *my* special department. Whenever I can save a Saturday for the farm, I try to give a good part of it to my patch of forest. The ax is the healthiest instrument that man ever handled, and is especially so for habitual writers, and other sedentary workers, whose shoulders it throws back, expanding their chests and opening their lungs. If every youth and man, from fifteen to fifty years old, could wield an ax two hours per day, dyspepsia would vanish from the earth, and rheumatism become decidedly scarce. I am a poor chopper; yet the ax is my doctor and delight. Its use gives the mind just enough occupation to prevent it falling into reverie or absorbing trains of thought, while every muscle in the body receives sufficient yet not exhausting exercise. I wish all our boys would learn to love the ax.

A Peck of Dirt.—Under this title, and in reference to the above, the periodical known as *Once a Week* has the following editorial comments, reminding the reader that the worst atmosphere we poor mortals have to breathe is *about five feet above the surface of the earth:*

Some few months ago D⁻. Letheby made known the results of various analyses of London mud, and told us that it contained fifty-seven per cent. of horse refuse, thirty per cent. of abraded stone, and thirteen per cent. of abraded iron from horses' hoofs and wheel tires. This delectable compound, rising in the form of dust in dry weather, is inhaled by passengers through the streets of the metropolis. A Dublin chemist, at about the same time, made similar revelations concerning the detritus of his city. Now we have the results of a microscopical examination of the solid particles that float in the air of Manchester. Mr. Dancer has been collecting these from various localities, and at different heights from the ground, and subjecting them to close scrutiny. As might be expected, various places and altitudes give atoms differing in magnitude, appearance and quantity per cubic inch of atmosphere. Strangely enough, the largest are found at about five feet from the ground, just the height of pedestrians' mouths; and the matter, chiefly vegetable, is that which has passed through the stomachs of animals, or which has suffered partial decomposition in some way or other. Sometimes animalculæ are present in good proportion. This is all very disagreeable; it is to be feared that they who dwell in dusty towns eat considerably more than the prescribed peck of dirt before they die. Whether they are worse for the excess remains to be proved; if they think that they are, let them go in for respirators and sift their oxygen.

Ventilation of Ferry-Boats.—This is an urgent necessity. We do not see any such packing together of human beings as on the Ferry-Boats. The stench in the saloons is beyond description. A writer in the *Brooklyn Union* discourses on this subject as follows, under date of February 11, 1867:

Now that the ferry question is being agitated, will you allow me to say a word in regard to the ventilation of the boats? Pure air costs nothing, though the extreme economy with which some people use it would lead us to believe it to be the most costly necessity that the world demands. We may search in vain for the smallest opening in the cabins of our ferry-boats; all the oxygen to be obtained crowds in at the door-seams, notwithstanding these boats are admirably adapted to the purposes of ventilation. The foulness of the air in the Fulton Ferry cabins at any hour of the night is overpowering; it is an absolute stench; every drawn breath is a death dart. There are not a few who, crossing late at night, and fatigued, prefer standing in the open air to sitting in these Vulcan's stithies. If we can not have many other things, we have a right to demand fresh air.

Ventilated Smoking-Rooms—Gen. Grant—Carlyle —Alice Cary.—The true gentleman will not smoke in the presence of others without first obtaining their consent. He knows that tobacco smoke is a poison to those not accustomed to the use of tobacco. He will therefore be considerate, and avoid making others sick by the indulgence of his habit. When you see a man smoking in an omnibus, or on the platform of a car, you may know that he is destitute of all the refining influences of society. Gen. Grant is a smoker, but he does not disregard the laws of decency in yielding to the habit. Mr. Carlyle is a smoker, but instead of polluting his house with tobacco smoke, he goes into his little flower garden in the rear of his house for that purpose. Here he smokes "his evening pipe," without offending any body's nostrils but his own, excepting those who may voluntarily seek an audience with him. In a notice of a "Woman's Club" in this city, of which Alice Cary is president, it was suggested, in reference to the accommodation of male visitors, that they should do their smoking in the attic. This would be well in one particular; no one would be made sick by the tobacco-smoke but the smokers themselves. But it would be cruel to banish the gentlemen visitors to the attic. Besides, "it is very bad," says the notice from which we quote, "for men to be much together. As they grow gregarious they are apt to grow coarse, and to be satisfied with a low standard of conversation. They talk horse, they talk dog, they talk wine, and they talk worse; they tell broad stories, and they crack broad jokes; they try to get away from commercial topics, or politics, and lamentably fail; they find each other inexpressibly stupid, and muddle themselves in the desperate effort to be sociable."

Smoking is beset with many difficulties. It not only offends your neighbor or friend, who is not accustomed to it, but it slowly and surely impairs the health. It pervades and saturates every part of the physical system. Cannibals in the South Sea Islands, it is said, will not eat the bodies of missionaries whom they have killed, in case the latter have been addicted to the use of tobacco. The flesh, impregnated with tobacco, is unsavory to the cannibal taste

Gentlemen who smoke, should have ventilated smoking-rooms in their houses. The smoke would then be carried away without saturating the house, or offending individuals in other rooms. Moreover, the smoking-room need not be in the attic, as mentioned above—it may be in the basement as well. Without ventilation, the concentrated smoke of tobacco, in a close room, becomes extremely disagreeable to the smokers themselves. The only remedy therefore is a *ventilated smoking-room*

WAS IT THE WHISKEY?—A gentleman came to us recently to talk ventilation. He had been getting some new ideas about foul air. He lived in the vicinity of Steinway Hall, and as the entertainments of the place were exactly suited to his taste, he was a frequent visitor at the Hall. But he never went there without getting a headache. Somebody told him it was the foul air. But he didn't believe it. He thought it was the whiskey he was in the habit of taking. Of course he wanted to explain about the whiskey. He wasn't a toper—nor was he a member of a temperance society. He had a trouble of the lungs, and his doctor thought a little whiskey would do him good. He didn't care much for the whiskey, but it wasn't hard to take, and so he swallowed a little of it now and then—a table-spoonful or so. He finally concluded that his headaches at Steinway Hall were caused by the whiskey, and not by the foul air, and so he left off the whiskey. He then went to the Hall on three different occasions without having taken any whiskey, and every night he had a headache just the same as before—worse and worse. He then concluded not to stop the whiskey any longer, but to stop going to Steinway Hall. He has not been to the Hall since, and don't intend to go any more, unless Mr. Steinway should have it ventilated. He don't believe in paying a dollar, or a dollar and half, for a headache. He thinks Mr. Steinway would be unreasonable to expect it.

COFFINS VERSUS VENTILATION.—Coffins cost money—so does ventilation. We sometimes think people would rather pay bills for coffins than to expend a little money for ventilation and fresh air. We have in our "mind's eye" a certain building that will serve for an illustration. Its whereabouts must remain a secret for the present. It is devoted to charitable purposes, and among other uses, it accommodates a Sunday-school, numbering 600 or 700 pupils, with thirty or forty lady teachers. The atmosphere of the school is extremely foul, and dangerous to health and life. It has been in this condition for a year and a half, notwithstanding the earnest remonstrances of the teachers, who are ladies of education and refinement, and whose lives are too valuable to be lost by such a reckless exposure to foul air. Large sums of money have been paid out for *tinkering projects* in the way of ventilation, but without the slightest success. Ladies frequently go home sick from the school. One lady was attacked with consumptive symptoms, and was brought to death's door, but slowly recovered. Healthy men are sometimes made sick by an exposure of an hour or two in the atmosphere of this building. We must now make a special application of our text, *coffins versus ventilation*. One of the prominent gentlemen having control of the above building, said that money could not be spared for its ventilation. Another gentleman, also interested in the building, hearing the remark, said, "Can't spare money to ventilate the building, sir? I want you to understand that we consider your life and services valuable, and if you are much exposed to the poisoned air of this building, you will die—you can't help it; and if you die, it will cost us at least $500 to bury you. If you care anything about your life, and wish to be economical, you had better pay the $500 for ventilation, or three times that amount, if necessary, and save your life. We wouldn't like to bury you, sir, for the sake of saving even fifteen hundred dollars." Thus ended the colloquy, and whether *coffins* or *ventilation* will carry the day, remains yet to be seen.

FURNACE HEAT DETRIMENTAL TO HEALTH.—Upon this important subject a correspondent of the *New York Times*, signing himself *Hygiene*, uses the following language:

The several articles which you have published lately upon the subject of furnace air, and the difficulty of sufficiently, and at the same time healthfully, heating our dwelling-houses, have been read with great interest and approval by many. The subject is certainly one of vast importance, and those who use furnaces, even for heating their halls only, should guard with the utmost care against the impure and injurious air which will be produced by *any* furnace not properly constructed and managed. That dry, almost choking air, which all must at times have perceived, is a promient cause of the colds so common, one might say universal, at the present day. The lungs are filled with it the greater portion of the time, and as a natural consequence, become weak and often diseased. When cold fresh air enters such sensitive organs, inflammation is frequently excited, and this, if often repeated, may result in consumption. Several of our leading physicians declare that three-fourths of the colds which prevail in all great cities during winter, early spring, and late fall, are caused by the unwholesome air produced by furnaces.

If you, by agitating the subject, and presenting it to the public in the *Times*, can persuade some of our scientific men to examine the matter, and produce a remedy for this evil, you will indeed be very great benefactors of your fellow-citizens.

The editor of the *Times*, in referring to the above article, indulges in the annexed comments:

A correspondent, whose letter we printed yesterday, thinks that we might do a great deal of good by running a-muck at the "furnace in the household." He would know better if he ever properly gauged the difficulty of breaking down old-established prejudices. People have got used to the heater, and they persuade themselves that they can not live without it. As a matter of fact, it is wonderful that they can live *with* it: the dry air is highly injurious to the constitution, and lays more children on sick beds at this season of the year than any other single cause. The first order a doctor gives when he enters a sick room, which is warmed by a heater, is for more ventilation. Poverty of blood, excessive liability to cold, feverishness, dry skin—these are the inevitable consequences of living in the unnatural atmosphere which we now find in nine houses out of ten. An open fireplace produces a draft up the chimney, and so ventilates the apartment. Moreover, a mere look at a blazing fire does more to warm and cheer one than all the steampipes ever made. But our correspondent "Hygiene" need not suppose that such considerations as these will change fixed habits.

OUR PASSENGER STEAMERS—THEIR GLORY AND THEIR SHAME.—Under this title the *New York Times*, in still another utilitarian article in relation to pure air and ventilation, has some remarks upon the subject of North River and other steamers, of which the annexed paragraph is an interesting sample:

In the matter of passenger comfort, the appointments of our steamers below deck are wholly inconsistent with the provisions for luxury above. The chief defect is the want of ventilation in the dining-saloon and in the adjacent staterooms. The greater number of passengers—at least those who have a sanitary, not to say æsthetical, idea of dining—habitually avoid the cabin of a steamboat, and so decrease the revenues of the Company, not because the cuisine or attendance is specially bad, but simply because the air of the saloon is intolerably hot for four months of the season, and insufferably foul from the opening to the closing of navigation. All this might be remedied by means of a ventilating fan. If great coal mines, hundreds of feet under ground, with narrow entrances choked with miasmatic and explosive gases, are kept wholesome and safe by single fans, certainly the cabin of a steamer, full of port-holes and skylights, may be kept pure and cool by similar means. A single fan, drawing out the foul air, and keeping a gentle current of fresh air passing through the cabin, would make it a most comfortable and desirable retreat, rather than a sweltering hole, which all men avoid if possible, and where the hungry bolt their food in order to make a speedy escape. We venture to say that the whole first cost of the apparatus, and the expenses of running it for an entire season, would be saved out of the increased dining-room profits of a single month. It rarely occurs that so great a luxury can be provided at so small a cost, and we urge our steamboat managers, now refitting their "floating palaces" for next season's business, not to overlook this signal means of augmenting their revenues and accommodating the traveling public.

The *ventilating fan*, spoken of above, will probably not be found a very serviceable fixture for ventilating purposes. It is neither efficient nor economical. If it answers no better in a steamboat than it has answered in the Capitol at Washington, and other public buildings, it will not amount to much. Air can be made to pass into and out of the cabin of a steamboat, for the purpose of ventilation, by a much more simple method than that of the fan arrangement. (See "Forced Ventilation," page 142)

"LITTLE NELLIE IS DYING !"—This was the mournful expression of an agonized mother to her family physician as he entered the parlor on a professional visit to her sick daughter, named above. "Little Nellie," as she was called, was not quite twelve years old, and was the darling child of her mother. Her history is brief. She had been sent to a public school, was studious and precocious, and always stood at the head of her class. Her health, however, was not good. She frequently came home from school with a headache ; and after a while she began to lose her appetite, and to look pale and haggard ; and still later, a cough began to trouble her, and the family physician advised her to give up study and stay away from school. Her cough increased, and it was not long before it was decided that little Nellie had the consumption. She was put into one of the best rooms of her mother's house, which was heated by a furnace ; and to keep out the fresh air as much as possible, through fear that it might be injurious to Nellie, the doors and windows were rendered air-tight by *weather-strips*. Every evening, as soon as the sun went down, Nellie's room was brilliantly lighted by the Argand burners of an elegant chandelier. This was for the purpose of rendering the apartment cheerful, according to the mother's idea, and to compensate, as far as possible, for the absence of the sun's rays. Many little girls of about Nellie's age, together with a number of her Sunday-school teachers, came very often to see her, and they were generally admitted into her room, sometimes a number of them together. It did not occur to any body that the furnace heat, the weather-strips, and the Argand burners, together with the presence of numerous visitors in the sick-room, all tended to render the atmosphere impure and deleterious.

We will now return to the mother and physician whom we left in the parlor. The mother, with tears gathering in eyes, said, "Do you think, doctor, that health is ever injured by foul air ?"

"Foul air !" repeated the doctor, with a look of astonishment. "What do you mean by foul air, madam?"

The mother replied, "I mean the air we breathe; is it not rendered foul by breathing it over a number of times?"

"I suppose it is," said the doctor, "but not in a sufficient degree to injure the health."

"You may not be sure of that," replied the mother. "I have heard of a place in India into which a number of men were crowded in the evening, with little or no fresh air, and in the morning the most of them were found dead."

"Oh," said the doctor, "that was the Black-Hole of Calcutta ;* such instances of exposure to foul air are very rare."

"It is to be hoped so," said the mother ; "but I fear, from all I have heard recently, that we have analagous *black-holes* in our very midst without recognizing the fact. If the men who died in India were destroyed by poisoned air in a few hours, why may not air less poisonous produce its effects upon the system more slowly, and give rise to sickness and ultimate death, while we are ignorant of the true cause of the difficulty?"

"It may be possible," replied the doctor, as if not disposed to continue the conversation.

"The subject is new to me," continued the mother, "but I consider it one of great importance. I have heard that there is a great deal of foul air in the public schools, owing to the absence of ventilation, and that teachers as well as pupils die in a short time of consumption, as a consequence of the foul air. I can now understand why my darling Nellie hardly ever came home from school without a headache;

---

* This was a dungeon, eighteen feet square, with only two small windows, into which 146 Englishmen were thrust. In less than an hour their breathing became difficult, and their cries for water were dreadful. Within three hours the most of them were dead. At six the next morning, making a period of twelve hours, an order came for their release, when only twenty-three of them were found alive. The most of these were prostrated with a putrid fever.

and if I had known that her health was in danger, nothing could have induced me to send her to school a single day."

"The air in our public schools is not as good as it ought to be," said the doctor.

"But the school," continued the mother, "has not been the only difficulty in my daughter's case. Through my ignorance of the laws of health, she has been shut up in a close room in which the air was nearly or perhaps quite as impure as that of her school-room. I excluded the fresh air with weather-strips; I depended for warmth upon furnace-heat, which I now understand is injurious to healthy people, to say nothing of invalids; I lighted the room with a number of Argand burners, to render it cheerful, which caused a large accummulation of what you doctors and chemists call carbonic acid gas, and which, I am told, is dangerous to health. There was no outlet to my daughter's room, excepting when the door was open, so that the poison of her breath, and the poison escaping from the lungs of her attendants and visitors, had no chance of making its escape. The sense of smell alone assured me that the air was very foul whenever I entered the room; but I supposed, in my ignorance, that the fresh air would be very injurious to my darling child. I see now, when it is too late, how great has been my error. The process of poisoning my child commenced at the public school, and I have completed it in my own house. The knowledge which I have obtained in relation to this matter was derived from a lady friend who called here by accident yesterday, and who had been in the army among our sick and wounded soldiers, where she acquired many useful lessons in relation to health and disease, and where, in particular, she had an opportunity of witnessing the baneful effects of foul air. But I am detaining you too long, doctor; my daughter can not live beyond another day, and I am not aware that your professional services can be of any further avail."

The doctor, who had listened to the mother with a saddened expression of countenance, attempted no reply, but moved quietly out of the parlor, and with a formal but respectful bow, made his exit from the house.

At the time of this conversation, little Nellie had been removed from the close room in which she had been long confined, without any remonstrance on the part of her physician to another apartment which had been hastily fitted up for her reception. This had been done at the instance of the lady-friend, spoken of in the preceding conversation. The room was heated by a stove instead of the furnace, and everything had been contrived, as well as it could be in so short a time, to furnish an agreeable atmosphere to the suffering patient. Little Nellie recognized the change at once, and said, "I seem to be in a new world, mamma." She then went to sleep, and waking, much refreshed, after a few hours, she looked up into her mother's face and said, "I breathe freely now ; I do not cough in this room as I did in the other ; I feel as if a heavy weight had been taken from my lungs ; I shall die easily ; death will come to me like a sweet sleep, or a sweet dream, and I shall only be sorry, dear mamma, to fly away to the land of spirits and leave you all alone."

Upon the utterance of these words the street door-bell rung, and presently the name of the family physician was announced. The heart-stricken mother, with her eyes filled with tears, went below into the parlor to receive her professional visitor. The conversation that ensued is recorded above.

INFANTILE DISEASE AND MORTALITY—FOUL AIR.— Dr. Meredith Clymer, American editor of an English work entitled *Principles of Medicine*, by Professor Williams, F. R. S., says in a note, "One of the most fertile sources of infantile disease is a want of pure and wholesome air, the effects of which are sure to manifest themselves, though often obscurely and at a remote period. It is physiologically impossible for human beings to grow up in a sound and healthy condition of body and mind, in the midst of a close, ill-ventilated atmosphere. Those that are least able to resist its baleful influence are carried off by the diseases of infancy and childhood ; and those whose native vigor of constitution enables them to struggle through these become the victims, in later years, of diseases which cut short their term of life, or deprive them of a large portion of that enjoyment which health alone can bring." . . . Dr. Clymer adds, "At the end of the last century, in the Dublin Foundling Hospital, during a space of twenty-one years, out of 10,272 sick children sent to the infirmary, only forty-five recovered. Deficient ventilation, from the crowding of the wards, was an efficient agent in this fearful result."

FARADAY's OPINIONS. — Who has not heard of Sir Michael Faraday, the eminent chemist? And who will not have a regard for his opinions on the subject of impure air and ventilation? The following remarks by him were made to a parliamentary committee in 1835, on the subject of ventilation. He said, "Air feels unpleasant in the breathing cavities, including the mouth and nostrils, not merely from the absence of oxygen, the presence of carbonic acid, or the elevation of temperature, but from other causes, depending on matters which are communicated to it by the human being. I think that an individual may find a decided difference in his feelings when making part of a large company, from what he does when one of a small number of persons, and yet the thermometer give the same indication. When I am one of a large number of persons, I feel an oppressive sensation of closeness, notwithstanding the temperature may be about 60° or 65°, which I do not feel in a small company at the same temperature, and which I can not refer altogether to the absorption of oxygen, or the evolution of carbonic acid, and which probably depends on the effluvia of the many present; but with me it is much diminished by a lowering of the temperature, and the sensations become much more like those occurring in a small company. The object of a good system of ventilation is to remove the effects of such air."

FAINTING AND HYSTERICS IN CHURCHES.—Dr. Combe, whose works have been so deservdly popular with the public, says, "Fainting and hysterics occur in churches much more frequently in the afternoon than in the forenoon, because the air is then vitiated to the full extent by breathing."

INFANT MORTALITY.—On this subject Dr. Combe further says: "About one hundred years ago, when the pauper infants of London were confined in the workhouses amid impure air, not more than one in twenty lived to be a year old, so that out of 2,800 received into them, 2,690 died yearly ; but when the conditions of health came to be better

understood, and an Act of Parliament was obtained, compel-
ling the parish officers to send the infants to nurse in the
country, this frightful mortality was reduced to 450
annually."

DR. THOMAS LAYCOCK — FOUL AIR — TYPHUS FEVER,
ETC.—The words of this celebrated English physician, as
recorded in the *London Medical Gazette*, will, no doubt, be
received as good authority everywhere. He says, "Under
the streets of our best-drained towns and cities there is a
widely-extended magazine of miasmata. That magazine is
hidden from view, yet it is ubiquitous. It enters every
court and alley, and during the heat of summer is put into
fearful activity, and night and day evolves many thousand cubic inches of foul air. And that foul air is often
imperceptible to the senses. Nobody suspects it is evolved
and ascends from every gully-hole, until previously to or
during rain, when it is held in solution in the aqueous vapor
of the atmosphere, and becomes perceptible to the sense of
smell. . . . Night and day a miasm is ascending from
the cess-pool called the street-drain, through the sink-hole
in the kitchen, and infecting the air of the whole house.
. . . It may have no smell, or no unpleasant smell.
and yet be a deadly poison. There is no smell in pure carbonic acid gas, and it is only an innocent odor of garlic that
characterizes the fumes of arsenic, yet both these are deadly
things. . . . I hold it to be an established principle
that the malaria arising from the abominable sewers, especially in the metropolis, [London,] where water-closets and
crowded church-yards abound, is the fruitful source of our
summer epidemics; and you may rely upon this, that
wherever you have cholera or typhus epidemic, there you
have a source of malaria. . . . When you find a
family suffering from cholera, or fever, you will find a filthy
drain close by."

Malaria.—In connection with the above, Dr. Laycock's
remarks upon the subject of malarious poisons are worthy
of special notice. He says, "I am inclined to think that
the excretions of swine and of human beings give off the
worst. I speak now of the source of civic malaria, and
not of malaria generally; otherwise the miasms from salt-
water marshes are perhaps worse than these. The next in

virulence are putrid water-butts and cisterns of water-closets, and emanations from water-closets themselves. Then the emanations from sewers, especially if connected with burial-grounds or slaughter-houses. Indeed, these latter belong to the first rank. Heaps of cow-dung or horse-dung are less injurious than the preceding, and chandleries follow after these. Sometimes cellars get flooded after heavy rains, and in summer send up a foul, damp miasm, and this is bad. You must remember that the general tendency of these miasms is to ascend. When the wind blows up or down the river [Thames] with force, I suspect it blows the miasm up the mouths of the drains which open into it. There is a back air as well as a back water, and this escapes through the gully-holes in the course of the sewer."

COWS AND COW STABLES.—WHAT A PROFESSOR OF MATERIA MEDICA SAYS. — Every thing pertaining to the cow is intimately related to the comfort and health of the human family, inasmuch as the milk of the cow is an indispensable article of diet. We have said elsewhere that a cow can not yield pure or wholesome milk unless she has pure air to breathe, and therefore the barbarous custom of shutting up cows in filthy and unventilated stables should be regarded as a crime punishable by statute. A case in point occurred in Brooklyn, where a cruel man shut up his cows in a stable, situated in Skillman Street, without light or ventilation. He was charged with cruelty to the animals, and had a hearing before Justice Cornwell. During the trial the following testimony was given by Dr Samuel R. Percy. We copy from the *New York Times* :

Q. What would be the effect upon cows confined in a dark, badly ventilated stable, in narrow stalls, chained so that their heads could only move about six inches, kept in that position for many months and fed upon soft food? *A.* The first effect on the animals would be to produce an uneasy, feverish state, with a loathing and rejection of food. This feverish state would last more or less during the confinement of the animal. At length a toleration of its circumstances would be acquired, so that the animal might live and yet not be healthy. Within a week or so after its confinement, another symptom, soreness of the feet, would occur—the feet would become tender, and he had seen hundreds of cases where the poor animal kept constantly changing its position on account of the tenderness and soreness of its feet. If the animal is long confined in such stables, the hoofs become elongated and the animal is thrown back upon the heel ; that has been noticed in a number of cases. He had seen animals of this description unfastened and let out. The effect is the same for a time after they get out on the ground – a constant lifting of the feet and a constant change of position. The animals also became sore by lying down. He had seen many sores left by sloughs, in the same way as bed-sores, by the animals lying down for ease. The effect of the air in these cases would be very deleterious, leading to impurity of the blood. So injurious had he seen this effect of bad air, that he had seen rows of cattle breathing over one hundred times a minute, while naturally they should breathe about twenty. The effect of the rapid breathing is to increase the frequency of the heart-beats till they become so rapid that it is impossible to count them. This must produce a general fever. Another disease produced by herding cows together in confined places is to give them what is called the "Distemper," which all cows take in these stables, unless vaccinated to prevent it. This vaccination is a cruel practise, causing the tail of the poor animal to swell, to become extremely sore, and frequently to compel the amputation of the tail to save the cow from death. It is this practice which has given the characteristic name of "stump-tails." (The witness here spoke about the cow-stables in Holland, where diseases were engendered by the close confinement of cattle, and thence spread, not only throughout Europe, but in this country, and he contended that thousands have died from diseases of the nature thus described.)

VOICE FROM JUDGE DIKEMAN.—The following letter from Judge Dikeman, in reference to the non-ventilation of his court-room, will explain itself, and has, we may add, a wide range of application :

BROOKLYN, April 24, 1867.

To the Honorable Board of Supervisors of Kings County :

The undersigned beg leave to say that, deeply impressed with the duty of affording persons charged with crime in said county a speedy trial, and of lessening as much as possible the expense of the county in jurors' fees, the Court of Sessions has from time to time for some years, and continuously since October last until about three weeks since, been usually held for five days in the week and for five to seven hours each day.

This service has been performed under the most unfavorable circumstances, and is extremely injurious to our health and the health of the jurors and others, arising from the want of suitable heat in cold weather and imperfect ventilation at all times.

That our experience has demonstrated to our entire satisfaction that without better ventilation we can not, with due regard to our health and the health of others, hold the Court of Sessions in the room now used for the purpose more than two hours each day—one hour in the morning and one hour in the afternoon—giving time for ventilation by opening the doors and windows between these times.

We have therefore, after mature deliberation, determined that we will not hold said Court in the room more than two hours in any one day. We regret the necessity of this determination, especially in view of the increased expenses which must result to the county for jurors' fees and the support of prisoners detained in jail awaiting trial.

Yours respectfully, JOHN DIKEMAN,

County Judge.

W. H. HOYT,

STEPHEN J. VOORHEES,

Associate Justices.

GOING TO SLEEP IN CHURCH—REV. THEODORE CUYLER.
—The *Brooklyn Union* for April 1, 1867, in a wide-awake
article upon the subject of church-ventilation, deliberately
places before its readers the following revolutionary statements and opinions :

Yesterday morning the Rev. Theodore Cuyler delivered a sermon in his
church, in Lafayette Avenue, in which he made allusion to those who go to
sleep in church. He regarded the custom of taking one's seat in a church and
preparing one's self for a cozy nap during the service as an insult to the
Almighty. That this habit of napping in church is objectionable there is no
doubt, but Mr. Cuyler should first realize, by experience, the impossibility of sitting in a pew of a heated and badly-ventilated building, without feeling a drowsiness come over him, before he preaches against a custom which nine out of ten
of those who fall asleep follow, not from choice, but from physical inability to keep
awake in an atmosphere where carbon is in the ascendant, and oxygen finds but
little chance of access. Last night in the gallery of the Lafayette Avenue church
people were fanning themselves to circulate air to breathe; and, as the doors
were closed, and but one small aperture in one of the windows was opened to
admit oxygen, and that, too, after a mild spring day, it was but little wonder
that drowsiness prevailed, although the sermon was interesting enough to keep
the dullest ear attentive. If you want your congregation to keep awake, ye
preachers who complain of sleepers, keep your churches well ventilated, and
not closed to the admission of oxygen, as the majority of them generally are.

BROOKLYN CHURCHES, ETC. — The *Brooklyn Union*,
quoted above, evidently does not intend to allow the
churches to have much rest until they decide to furnish
to their congregations a better atmosphere than they have
at present. It frequently has editorials in reference to
church, as well as school ventilation. We copy below a
communication addressed to the editor of the *Union*, headed
" Ventilation of Churches," and signed S. B. C.

In this Augustan age it would seem that science and sense should deal with
matters that pertain to the human race, and that evils flagrant in character
should be banished from our midst. Yet, in spite of the teachings of the past,
we still wander on in the same beaten track, and are content with the old *regime*.
The doctors all agree in saying that the breathing of impure air is a common source
of disease. Now I think it would be difficult to find a single church in our city
that is properly ventilated. To attend service on Sunday night is to injure one's
health. Before the evening is half gone all interest in the sermon subsides, the
gas grows dim, and the close of the meeting is anxiously looked for. In the
construction of new buildings the laws of health should be consulted. It would
be a very easy matter to correct the present ill-devised mode of ventilation, and
thereby insure comfort to church-goers. A reform is much needed, and certainly a beginning should be made.

A PROTEST TO MR. BEECHER.—A writer, with a somewhat caustic pen, addresses the following letter to the Rev.
Mr. Beecher, (Henry Ward, we presume,) through one of

the public journals, and signs himself, " Your loving but greatly distressed Hearer."

My Dear Brother Beecher: I take great pleasure in saying that I attended your lecture delivered last evening before the Christian Medical Association, and was charmed and delighted with its freshness and pointed practicalness. The home-thrusts at the politico-sanitary management of these two great cities, the medico-politico metaphors, such as the great systems of veins and arteries (sewers) reeking with poison which they distributed to the destruction of the lives of our citizens, capital hits at our ignorance of the laws of dietetics and hygiene, and most pungent admonitory thrusts at the profession because they did not undertake an active crusade against all these crying evils.

All this was splendid and soul-satisfying, but, my dear and reverend brother, with your clairvoyant spirit, were you not conscious that all the while you were thus spending your electric power upon your vast audience, at least one half of it were suffering the torture of slow poison from one of the sources against which you were most loudly inveighing, to wit, bad ventilation? For one, I was obliged to put forth my utmost power, although extremely interested in the discourse, to prevent somnolency. Others around me in the gallery complained in the same manner.

The old adage, "Charity begins at home," it seems to me, should have its exemplification just here. And to this end I, with a thousand more miserable suffering sinners, beg that you will immediately stir up—with a very acutely acuminated stick — the pure minds of your trustees, that they may at once set their house in order in this respect; for by doing so they will most assuredly save many bodies, if not souls, from death, and cover up a multitude of sins, or, at least, save a multitude from breaking the commandment against cursing.

BEECHER AND THE MEDICAL PROFESSION.—The "distressed hearer," quoted in the last article, had reference to a discourse delivered by Mr. Beecher before the New York Medical Students' Christian Union, February 3d, 1867, at Plymouth Church, Brooklyn. We find it reported in the *Herald of Health* for April, 1867. Here are a few piquant extracts. Mr. Beecher remarks that "it is a part of the business of the medical profession to teach the great truths which stand connected with health in the matter of air and light," and then proceeds as follows in relation to the foul air of houses, steamboats, churches, etc.

The principal use which men seem to put air to is to destroy it. They go into their houses and shut out the exterior air, and burn by stoves that which is inside, and poison it by breathing, and then, when it is thoroughly destructive, go on breathing it, and sucking it in, as if it were a confection, or a luxury! Is there any body that teaches men what air means when applied to travel in steamboats? It is enough to set one to retching just to remember the cabin! Is there any body to teach the community the benefit of air in railway cars, in churches, in lecture-halls, in places of crowded assembly? We should scorn with ineffable scorn to sit down at a plate where a man had just eaten his meal, and take the knife that had been in his mouth and put it in ours; but we will sit down and breathe the air that he has breathed, and that his wife has breathed, and that his children have breathed, and that the servants have breathed, and that forty others have breathed, and will think it just as good for our breathing, and will breathe it over, and over, and over again, as if it was a precious morsel! There seems to be no power to impress men that God made pure air for promoting health, and that impure air produces the crime of sickness—for I think that sickness is a sin.

"Snuff in Sermons."—One of our city dailies uses this expression in a notice of *Packard's Monthly*, and says it "seems to have adopted the spicy sensational style as a matter of principle. The editor has more faith in sharp, incisive thrusts than in sleepy, droning homilies. The means of grace, in his view, should be pungent, as well as pious. He likes the story of an old minister who advised his young clerical friend to put 'snuff in his sermons,' if he wished to keep the people awake, and confesses that he means to use that policy in the management of his magazine."

Instead of *snuff in sermons* to keep people awake, it will be found more efficient to supply the church with pure air. It is not easy to keep awake in an atmosphere poisoned by the human breath.

BODILY RELIGION—BY HARRIET BEECHER STOWE.

Mrs. Stowe is one of the celebrities of American literature. Who has not read her books? Who is not familiar with her name and fame? Many of her brilliant productions have been translated into foreign tongues, so that she is almost as well known upon the other side of the Atlantic as upon this. She is a woman of great practical good sense, and does not merely busy herself in writing agreeable or instructive works of fiction, but grapples also with subjects connected with our domestic and social welfare. In the *Atlantic Monthly* for July, 1866, is an article entitled "Bodily Religion," from the pen of Mrs. Stowe, in which she discusses the subject of foul air, lack of ventilation, and kindred topics, with a force and pungency which must win for her the admiration of every intelligent and utilitarian reader. The following extracts are from the *Atlantic Monthly*, as already indicated:

OUR PRETTY BOY.—Take our pretty boy, with cheeks like apples, who started in life with a hop, skip, and dance; to whom laughter was like breathing, and who was enraptured with plain bread and milk; how did he grow into the man who wakes so languid and dull, who wants strong coffee and Worcestershire sauce to make his breakfast go down? . . . What is the boy's history? . . . He is made to sit six hours a day in a close, hot room, *breathing impure air*, putting the brain and the nervous system upon a constant strain, while the muscular system is repressed to an unnatural quiet.

WANT OF VENTILATION IN SCHOOL-ROOMS.—The want of suitable ventilation in school-rooms, recitation-rooms, lecture-rooms, offices, court-rooms, conference-rooms and vestries, where young students of law, medicine, and theology acquire their earlier practice, is something simply appalling. Of itself it would answer for men the question, why so many thousand glad, active children come to a middle life without joy—a life whose best estate is a sort of slow, plodding endurance. The despite and hatred which most men seem to feel for God's gift of fresh air, and their resolution to breathe as little of it as possible, could only come from a long course of education, in which they have been accustomed to live without it. Let any one notice the conduct of our American people traveling in railroad cars. We will suppose that about half of them are what might be called well-educated people, who have learned in books, or otherwise, that the air breathed from the lungs is laden with impurities, that it is noxious and poisonous; and yet, travel with these people half a day, and you would suppose from their actions that they considered the external air as a poison created expressly to injure them, and that the only course of safety lay in keeping the cars hermetically sealed and breathing over and over the vapor from each others' lungs. If a person in despair at the intolerable foulness raises a window, what frowns from all the neighboring seats, especially from great rough-coated men, who always seem the first to be apprehensive! The request to "put down that window" is almost sure to follow a moment or two of fresh air.

FOUL AIR OF COURT ROOMS.—We have spoken of the foul air of court-rooms. What better illustration could be given of the utter contempt with which the laws of bodily health are treated than the condition of these places? Our lawyers are our highly educated men. They have been through high school and college training, they have learned the properties of oxygen, nitrogen, and carbonic acid gas, and have seen a mouse die under an exhausted receiver, and of course they know that foul, unventilated rooms are bad for the health; and yet generation after generation of men so taught and trained will spend the greater part of their lives in rooms notorious for their close and impure air, without so much as an attempt to remedy the evil. A well-ventilated court-room is a four leaved clover among court-rooms. Young men are constantly losing their health at the bar; lung diseases, dyspepsia, follow them up, gradually snapping their vitality. Some of the brightest ornaments of the profession have actually fallen dead as they stood pleading—victims of the fearful pressure of poisonous and heated air upon the excited brain. The deaths of Salmon P. Chase, of Portland, uncle of our present Chief-Justice, and of Ezekiel Webster, the brother of our great statesman, are memorable examples of the calamitous effects of the errors dwelt upon; and yet, strange to say, nothing efficient is done to mend these errors, and give the body an equal chance with the mind in the pressure of the world's affairs.

FOOD AND FRESH AIR CONTRASTED—CHURCHES.—People would never think of bringing a thousand persons into a desert place, and keeping them there, without making preparations to feed them. Bread and butter, potatoes and meat, must plainly be found for them; but a thousand human beings are put into a building to remain a given number of hours, and no one asks the question whether means exist for giving each one the quantum of fresh air needed for his circulation; and these thousand victims will consent to be slowly poisoned, gasping, sweating, getting red in the face, with confused and sleepy brains, while a minister with a yet redder face and a more oppressed brain struggles and wrestles, through the hot, seething vapors, to make clear to them the mysteries of faith. How many churches are there that, for six or eight months in the year, are never ventilated at all, except by the accidental opening of doors? The foul air generated by one congregation is locked up by the sexton for the use of the next assembly; and so gathers and gathers from week to week, and month to month, while devout persons upbraid themselves, and are ready to tear their hair, because they always feel stupid and sleepy in church. The proper ventilation of their churches and vestries would remove that spiritual deadness of which their hymns and prayers complain. A man hoeing his corn out on a breezy hillside is bright and alert, his mind works clearly, and he feels interested in religion, and thinks of many a thing that might be said at the prayer-meeting at night. But at night, when he sits down in a little room where the air reeks with the vapor of his neighbor's breath and the smoke of kerosene lamps, he finds himself suddenly dull and drowsy—without emotion, without thought, without feeling—and he rises and reproaches himself for this state of things.

ARSENIC AND PRAYER-MEETING.—Suppose that a revival of religion required, as a formula, that all the members of a given congregation should daily take a minute dose of arsenic in concert, we should not be surprised after a while to hear of various ill effects therefrom; and, as vestries and lecture-rooms are now arranged, a daily prayer-meeting is often nothing more nor less than a number of persons spending half an hour a day breathing poison from each other's lungs. There is not only no need of this, but, on the contrary, a good supply of pure air would make the daily prayer-meeting far more enjoyable. The body, if allowed the slightest degree of fair play, so far from being a contumacious infidel or opposer, becomes a very fair Christian helper, and, instead of throttling the soul, gives it wings to rise to celestial regions.

TAVERN LIFE IN CONNECTICUT.—Let a person travel in private conveyance up through the valley of the Connecticut, and stop for a night at the taverns which he will usually find at the end of each day's stage. The bed-chamber into which he will be ushered will be the concentration of all forms of bad air. The house is redolent of the vegetables in the cellar—cabbages, turnips, and potatoes—and this fragrance is confined and retained by the custom of closing the window-blinds and dropping the inside curtains, so that neither air nor sunshine enters in to purify. Add to this the strong odor of a new feather-bed and pillows, and you have a combination of perfumes most appalling to a delicate sense. Yet travelers take possession of these rooms, sleep in them all night without raising the window or opening the blinds, and leave them to be shut up for other travelers.

EXPERIMENT IN CHURCH VENTILATION. — An energetic sister in the church suggested the inquiry, whether it was ever ventilated, and discovered that it was regularly locked up at the close of service, and remained so till opened for the next week. She suggested the inquiry, whether giving the church a thorough airing on Saturday would not improve the Sunday services; but nobody acted on her suggestion. Finally, she borrowed the sexton's key one Saturday night, and went into the church and opened all the windows herself, and let them remain so for the night. The next day every body remarked the improved comfort of the church, and wondered what had produced the change. Nevertheless, when it was discovered, it was not deemed a matter of enough importance to call for an order on the sexton to perpetuate the improvement.

RECEIPT FOR CONSUMPTION, DYSPEPSIA, ETC. — The spare chamber of many dwellings seems to be an hermetically closed box, opened only twice a year for spring and fall cleaning; but for the rest of the time closed to the sun and the air of heaven. Thrifty country housekeepers often adopt the custom of making their beds on the instant after they are left, without airing the sheets and mattresses; and a bed so made gradually becomes permeated with the insensible emanations of the human body, so as to be a steady corrupter of the atmosphere.

In the winter, the windows are caulked and listed, the throat of the chimney built up with a tight brick wall, and a close stove is introduced to help burn out the vitality of the air. In a sitting-room like this, from five to ten persons will spend about eight months of the year, with no other ventilation than that gained by the casual opening and shutting of doors. Is it any wonder that consumption every year sweeps away its thousands? that people are suffering constant chronic ailments, neuralgia, nervous dyspepsia, and all the host of indefinite bad feelings that rob life of sweetness, and flower, and bloom?

CHARLOTTE CUSHMAN AND DR. J. MARION SIMS — ERYSIPELAS—VENTILATION—WILLIAM PITT FESSENDEN —BY MORRIS MATTSON, M.D.

Charlotte Cushman is well known as a distinguished actress, whose Lady Macbeth and Meg Merrilies will not soon be forgotten by those who have witnessed the personations. Dr. Sims is equally well known as the originator of a new surgical operation, which has been of incalculable benefit to many suffering women, and he has now a trans-Atlantic as well as cis-Atlantic fame. . . . Miss Cushman was taken ill in September of this year (1869) which gave great concern to her numerous friends. In consequence of this illness, Dr. Sims addressed the following letter to the editor of the *New York Times*, dated October 3, 1869, which will explain itself:

The sad news given in yesterday's *Times* by your correspondent at Malvern in reference to the health of Miss Cushman, will carry sorrow to thousands of her friends here. It is to quiet all apprehensions of immediate danger that I venture to write these lines.

Miss Cushman called to see me in Paris on the 4th June last. She was in apparently vigorous health; yet she had for some time a little indurated gland that gave her great mental anxiety, but no physical suffering. I advised her to let it alone, to avoid all immediate surgical interference, to go to Malvern for the season, and to dismiss the subject from her thoughts.

It seems that she went to Malvern, but unfortunately she has submitted to extirpation of the gland. Now, what I wish to say is this:—There was no immediate danger in her disease, and there could be no sort of danger in the operation, *per se*, for it is one of the easiest and simplest in the whole range of surgery. As she was, on or before the 16th of September, (the date of your correspondent's letter,) lying "at the point of death, quite given up by her friends," I am pretty sure that the operation must have been followed by erysipelas, for from the very nature of the case, it is almost the only accident that could have happened. Now, erysipelas is a disease that would by self-limitation have terminated before this either in convalescence or death. And as we have received no news by telegram of the latter, the inference is clear to my mind that our gifted country woman is now convalescent. Let us then hope for the best till we know the worst.

The next public intelligence in relation to Miss Cushman was contained in a paragraph in the *Tribune* for November 27, which reads as follows:

Charlotte Cushman is recovering, and expects shortly to go to Rome. She writes from Edinburgh—"I am, thank God, able to drive out an hour each day in the sun, which feels very grateful to me. Each day, since I have had permission, I am gradually picking up under the influence of the air, from which I have been shut out for eight weeks—and eight weeks of such suffering."

What has this to do with ventilation? Much! The *Malvern* alluded to by Dr. Sims, contains a number of water-cures, into one of which, it is to be presumed, Miss Cushman went for treatment. Be it known, therefore, that water-cures, as well as hospitals, if not ventilated, are sure to become surcharged with foul air. . . . In September Miss Cushman was at the point of death, and Dr. Sims informs the public that this could not have been from the surgical operation, in which there was "no sort of danger," but from *erysipelas*, which he felt sure must have followed the operation. If, therefore, Miss Cushman's life was in danger from *erysipelas*, it is important that the public, for whose benefit water-cures and hospitals are instituted, should be informed in reference to the nature or character of the disease, especially as they are beginning to look a little more closely than heretofore into the rationale of *cause* and *effect*. It is known to physicians, though not perhaps to non-medical readers, that erysipelas is a well recognized *zymotic disease*, which results, as the name imports, from *foul air*, and that it is apt to follow surgical operations in hospitals, and similar places, as a consequence of the deleterious action of foul air. This is a fearful consideration, inasmuch as the disease occasions intense suffering, and also endangers human life. Miss Cushman, in her letter copied from the *Tribune*, speaks of the eight weeks of terrible suffering which she endured; and if we are to assume that this suffering was attributable to erysipelas, and that the erysipelas resulted from the foul air of the establishment or institution in which she had sought refuge, it is a fact that should never be overlooked or forgotten. It should be burnt into the memory so as never to be effaced. We can not afford to lose valuable lives, nor lives of any description, from ignorance or disregard of an unquestionable hygienic law. Miss Cushman tells the world that after her eight weeks of suffering she was gradually picking up under the influence of the *fresh air*, from which she had been excluded for so long a time. It was only by "permission," however, according to her own statement, that she was enjoying this grand luxury of a benificent Creator. But should there be any embargo upon fresh air? Is it not a medicine, or something better than a medicine, which every suffering invalid should be permitted to breathe without restriction? We have spoken of *cause* and *effect*. Let this be faithfully studied. Let it be understood that *foul air*, to which so little attention is given, is capable of rapidly destroying the health and prostrating the system, as seems to have been the case with Miss Cushman. Before going to Malvern, according to Dr. Sims, she was in "apparently vigorous health," and yet, in a brief period, she was brought to the verge of the grave. How long will the public have to wait before water-cures and hospitals are ventilated? Is it not a mockery to talk about the cure of disease so long as invalids are compelled to breathe a foul or mephitic atmosphere? Remember what Dr. Willard Parker has said about the cholera. Upon entering Bellevue Hospital in the mornings, he could not get along without stepping over dead bodies. In this extremity, he directed tents to be put up in the *open air*, and ordered "the poor fellows to take their chances" within these tents. Wonderful to tell, *every one of the patients got well.* This was a miracle in medical practice. Thus, we can not fail to perceive the difference between *fresh air* and *foul air.* Let us profit by the comparison, and learn wisdom by the experience.

Foul air not only rapidly prostrates the system, but its havoc is sometimes apparent for many subsequent years. In this connection we are reminded of the late WILLIAM PITT FESSENDEN, Senator from Maine. He died during the present year. In 1857, he was one of the victims of the *foul-air epidemic* in Washington, better known as the "National Hotel Epidemic." He escaped with his life, but it is said that he never wholly recovered from the prostrating effects of the illness.

MARK TWAIN ON "SMELLS," THE TURKISH BATH, ETC.— "SMELLS" IN CHICAGO AND NEW YORK.

Mark Twain is a well-known eccentric and comical genius, being a second edition of Artemus Ward. He has an odd way of telling homely truths, which impress themselves upon the public mind. He has written funny books, in which we wish him abundant success. He went off in the famous "Mediterranean Excursion" a few years ago, and has given the world an amusing record of his adventures. What he says upon the subject of *"Smells"* is worthy of special study, and we shall quote it for the benefit of those who don't believe in ventilation. Our traveler arrived at "Civita Vecchia the Forlorn," as he expresses it, on a sweltering day in July, and headed one of his unique letters, from which we are about to quote, "At Large in Italy." He says, "This is the vilest nest of dirt, vermin, and ignorance we have got into yet, except that African perdition they call Tangier, which is just like it. The people here live in alleys two yards wide. It is lucky the alleys are not wide, because they hold as much smell now as a person can stand; and, of course, if they were wider, they would hold more, and then the people would die. These alleys are paved with stone, carpeted with slush, decayed rags, decomposed vegetable tops, and remnants of old boots, all soaked with dish-water, and the people sit around on stools and enjoy it. They work two or three hours at a time, but not hard, and then they knock off and catch fleas. This does not require talent, because they have only to grab; if they don't get the one they are after, they get another. It is all the same to them. They are not particular."

Turkish Bath and Turkish Coffee.—Mark Twain heads another letter with the phrases, "A Yankee in the Orient," and "Poetical Humbuggery." This time he is in Constantinople. He says, "When I think how I have been swindled by books of Oriental travel, I want a tourist for breakfast. For years and years I have dreamed of the wonders of the Turkish Bath ; for years and years I have promised myself that I would yet enjoy one." But the picture, as he "got it from incendiary books of travel, was a poor, miserable fraud, the reality being no more like it than the Five Points are like the Garden of Eden." He was bent upon taking a bath, however, and passed into a great court, "furnished with huge, rickety chairs, cushioned with rusty old mattresses indented with impressions left by the forms of nine successive generations of men who had reposed upon them. The cadaverous, half-nude varlets that served in the establishment had nothing of poetry in their appearance, nothing of oriental splendor. They shed no entrancing odors—just the contrary."

Our adventurer was soon undressed, and then "an unclean starveling wrapped a gaudy table-cloth about his loins, and hung a white rag over his shoulders." Next in order, they gave him a pair of wooden clogs, which he calls "benches in miniature," and which "dangled uncomfortably by the leather straps when he lifted his feet." But these "sensuous influences," and this "oriental luxury," he did the best he could to enjoy.

The bath proceeding, our traveler was ushered into another department, in which he was "laid on a stuffy sort of pallet." This was a solemn place. He now expected that the spiced odors of Araby would steal over his senses, but they didn't. A copper-colored skeleton, with a rag around him, brought a decanter of water, with a lighted tobacco pipe on the top of it, and a pliant stem a yard long, with a brass mouth-piece to it. Our traveler took one blast at it, which was sufficient. The smoke all went down his throat. It came back in convulsive snorts through his nose. It had a vile taste ; and the mouth-piece tasted viler still, as well it might, for it had been in contact with a thousand infidel lips and tongues.

The critical portion of the bath was now ushered in—critical, we may call it, because there was a development of certain "smells," which our traveler tells us had none of the dreamy odors of Araby. He was stretched upon a raised platform, and goes on with his story as follows: "Presently my man sat me down by a tank of hot water, drenched me well, gloved his hand with a coarse mitten, and began to polish me all over with it. I began to *smell disagreeably.* The more he polished, the *worse I smelt.* It was alarming. I said to him, 'I perceive that I am pretty far gone. It is plain that I ought to be buried without any unnecessary delay. Perhaps you had better go after my friends at once, because the weather is warm, and I can not keep long.'"

No attention was paid to these entreaties. After a while the man brought a basin, some soap, and something that seemed to be the tail of a horse. He deluged our unfortunate traveler with soap-suds, without warning him to shut his eyes, and then swabbed him viciously with the horse-tail, until he became "a statue of snowy lather." After this, he was flooded with "exhausting hot water." In all this there seemed to be nothing of "oriental voluptuousness." After a while the "world-renowned Turkish-coffee, that poets have sung of so rapturously, was brought, but this also proved to be a swindle. Of all the unchristian beverages that ever passed the lips of our traveler, this Turkish coffee he considered the worst. The cup was small and smeared with grounds ; the coffee was black, thick, unsavory of smell, and execrable in taste. The bottom of the cup had a muddy sediment in it half an inch thick. Thus ended the celebrated Turkish Bath, and it is apparent that ventilation and fresh air are not appreciated by the Turks any more than the Christians.

"Smells in Chicago." — Our American Chicago is more than a match for the Italian Civita Vecchia in the way of *smells.* Our authority for this is the reporter of the *Chicago Tribune,* who made a memorable voyage up the

Chicago River, Anno Domini, 1868, and favored the world with the result of his observations. He is not inferior to Mark Twain in truthfulness and veracity, and therefore no one need doubt the correctness of his statements. He has furnished an elaborate Catalogue of 1,607 "well-defined and separate bad smells," which he detected during his remarkable river voyage. These smells, according to his showing, emanated "from distilleries, dead dogs, the carcasses of cats, tanneries, poisoned fish, malt from the breweries, the refuse of slaughter-houses, and contributions from the sewers." The *New York Tribune* says, "The only wonder experienced by us in reading the above report was that anybody should be alive in Chicago at this moment." The Chicago reporter has nothing to say about the *Chicago Court-House*, which should not have been overlooked. Had he visited the *Comptroller's Room* before we ventilated it (see page 159) he would have been enabled to increase his list of "well-defined bad smells."

"SMELLS" IN NEW YORK CITY.—It may be regarded as an unsettled question whether Civita Vecchia and Chicago, not to say anything about Mark Twain's African Tangier, is entitled to the palm of superiority over our goodly city in the score of bad smells and horrible stenches. There are some features of our metropolitan life which bid defiance to rivalship. We allude with great deference to the *bone-boiling establishments*, which now seem to be recognized as permanent institutions in our city. They are dealt with by the authorities very tenderly; and some of our learned and scientific men have assumed that the stenches from these establishments are not detrimental to the health at all, but are in reality very agreeable and wholesome odors. It may be that some industrious vender of perfumes will yet collect these odors, and sell them by the bottle, in place of Lubin's Extracts. Who knows? If they are really beneficial to the health, our city mortality should be greatly reduced below its present figures, especially in the upper portions of the city, where the fat-boiling stenches predominate. Without going further into this branch of our subject, we will direct attention very briefly to some of the additional smells and stenches of New York City and Brooklyn.

Sewer-Gas.—Under this head reference is made by the Board of Health, in one of its reports, to the sewer in West Forty-Second Street. This sewer, according to the report, "is above the low-water mark, and during the daily tidal fluctuations, emits the foulest and deadliest kind of sewer-gas."

Crossing the East River to Brooklyn, we will quote from the report of Dr. F. W. Colton, in relation to the sewer emptying into the East River at the foot of Atlantic Street. He says it discharges into the dock, where the water lies motionless, rendering the place a cess-pool, and impregnating the air with the most pestilential odors. He describes the effect of these exhalations upon the occupants of the Columbia Street stores, and says, "The employees of the Ferry are daily made sick in warm weather by inhaling the vitiated air; and passengers inhaling a deep breath before they enter the slip, do not breathe again until they have made their escape from the premises."

Almost the entire City of New York is sometimes pervaded by the smell of sewer-gas, which is sulphuretted hydrogen, and which is highly injurious to the health of the citizens, inasmuch as it is an intense blood poison.

Congregation of Bad Smells.—Here is a batch of nuisances, with their accompanying odors or stenches, which were abated in a single week, during April, 1866, in anticipation of the cholera. We quote from a report issued by the Board of Health. Such nuisances are constantly to be found in our city:

Filthy sinks and water-closets cleansed		605
Loads of night soil removed from city limits		2,009
Dead horses removed " "		72
" cows " " "		4
" goats " " "		6
" sheep " " "		18
" dogs and cats removed " "		38
" calves ("bobs") " " "		11

Cow-Stable Odors.—Here is what the Health Board said of a cow-stable, located at the time in West Forty-Eighth Street: "The stalls are disgustingly filthy, as well as the animals themselves. The manure hall emits a vile odor. The yard is filthy and wet, made so by the manure, urine and water." The milk of such cows as these, we may add, is constantly sold to the citizens of New York, and is literally a poison.

Crossing again to Brooklyn, we will quote from Dr. S. W. Fisk, who was Inspector of the Fourth Sanitary District, in reference to cow-stables. He says that the stables in First Street "are occupied by large numbers of cows of the stump-tail, swill-fed species, and are reeking with filth. The stalls are fearfully overcrowded, and the atmosphere is almost insupportable, no attention being paid to ventilation."

TENEMENT-HOUSE ABOMINATIONS—VENTILATION OF TENEMENT HOUSES.

The sanitary condition of New York tenement-houses is a reproach to our city, although it is claimed that they have been somewhat improved within a year or two through the instrumentality of the Board of Health. But they are still over-crowded, and still continue to be the abodes of poverty and misery, filth and rags. If they are better ventilated than heretofore, it is chiefly through open windows, which are not very efficient in supplying fresh air to the interior of a house, and which can not be used in winter without the risk of chilling or freezing the occupants. We have already stated that fresh air should be furnished to the poor, in their houses, even though they are deprived of every other comfort. This could be efficiently done without expending a large sum of money, and we predict that it would be a profitable investment. If the experiment of ventilating tenement-houses should be tried — we mean, of course, thorough and efficient ventilation—it will be found, when the matter is understood, that the rooms are more attractive to the poor, and will command better prices ; and if over-crowding is inevitable, which can not be prevented as long as there are poverty-stricken people seeking a home or a shelter, it may be a consolation to know that *twenty individuals* may be packed in a small room, during the hours of sleep, and yet have an ample supply of fresh air to breathe. Thus, the landlord would be amply remunerated for the expenditure of his money, and the occupants of the house would be vastly benefited by the new order of things.

With fresh air taking the place of mephitic gases and poisons, the over-crowded poor will be much less liable to sickness; they will be less exposed to the ravages of the zymotic diseases; they will not experience so intense a craving for spirituous liquors; they will attend to their labors or duties with more zeal and fidelity; and their general physical condition will be, in many particulars, essentially improved. These are important considerations. The experiment of tenement-house ventilation, therefore, ought to be tried the moment it can be done *properly* and *efficiently*, for we have no reference in these remarks to imperfect *window ventilation*, nor any of the modern *shams* which pass under the name of ventilation. The efficient ventilation of a single tenement-house would be a more important achievement than a score of lectures or written discourses on the value of fresh air without ventilation. Fifty thousand dollars expended by the city in properly ventilating tenement-houses would result in a heavy reduction of the poor tax, because it would prevent a large amount of sickness, and enable the tenantry to attend to their labors or business, and become thereby self-supporting, instead of becoming a public burthen in our alms-houses.

The reports of the Board of Health, and other similar documents, for the past two or three years, will suffice to show the wretched condition of our tenement-houses. Some of them may be in a better condition now than when the reports were made, but the aggregate of filth, and misery, and over-crowding, is probably much the same now as at any previous period. The following extracts are from various reports which lie upon our table:

A Nest of Foul Places.—We find a notice of these in the reports of Benjamin Warden, who was employed by the Board of Health during the cholera season of 1866. . . No. 54 Mulberry Street; a filthy, low den. . . . Cellars in Leonard and Baxter Streets; water coming through the floors, walls mouldy, ceilings all fallen down. . . . No. 41 Baxter Street, in the rear; very bad, stinks horribly. . . . No. 64 Cherry Street; very filthy, unfit for a dog to live in. . . . No. 103 Cherry Street; has eight beds in the front basement, ceiling low, not fit for a human habitation.

TENEMENT-HOUSES DESCRIBED.—In the *New York Tribune* for June 12, 1867, there is an able and interesting article in relation to the tenement-houses of our city by one of the reporters of that journal. Whether he is the author of the graphic report in relation to the Metropolitan School-Houses, from which we have made extracts, we are unable to say. He has, at all events, rendered the public a signal service by exposing some of the metropolitan horrors by which we are surrounded. Here are some descriptive remarks to which we invite the reader's special attention :

A FRIGHTFUL PICTURE.—Houses such as these, fitted only for the most destructive ferments known to medical experience, become human habitations. The largest number of families the building will hold is the smallest number with which the owner will be satisfied. The question as to how the different sexes will dispose of themselves, or how they will dispose of their filth, does not concern him in the least. In one of these houses so inhabited, privacy is unknown. The meanest offices of life and all the necessities of nature are unavoidably open to the gaze of both young and old, male and female alike. The stairways and halls are common to all occupants of the house, and are always filthy, for the reason that the duty which devolves upon everybody is performed by nobody. The sinks are continuously foul, and the water-closets, which all use, no one cleans. By-and-by these become unfit for use even by the most unclean, and in a short time the cellar is transformed into a cess-pool. The exhalations from this decomposing mass rise into the rooms of the sleepers and mix with an atmosphere already vitiated, and at least partially confined, making " the rankest compound of villainous smell that ever offended nostril." Every room in these houses is the ally of disease, and to many of the houses death is a weekly visitor. . . . Why all the inhabitants of this class of tenement-houses do not instantly die can only be accounted for upon the hypothesis that there is an occult law at work in an effort to adapt their internal relations to their surroundings.

We have given above an outline for which hundreds of houses in this city will furnish ample details. Indeed, there is an entire block of houses in Forty-Second Street, west of Eleventh Avenue, each one of which furnishes all the requirements of our description, save, perhaps, in height and depth. The buildings of which this block is composed are four stories high with a cellar under each one. The base of the cellar-floors was found to be an indescribable quagmire of filth, which oozed up between the boards as the visitors passed through. The ceilings are on a level with the street and scarcely more than six feet high—they can easily be touched by the hand—while the presence of fire-places and closets showed that the rooms had been intended for human habitations. The stench was intolerable, and when the floor was raised, became sickening. A man who had sounded this mass of liquid filth in one of the cellars told the writer that it was eighteen inches deep. The floors in some of the cellars, and in all of the closets, save those which had been recently cleaned, were defiled by human excrement. The walls were dirty in the extreme, and the stairs boken down and dilapidated. Each house visited presented the same general characteristics, the only difference seeming to be in the amount of filth and the disagreeableness of odors.

A Stench that Makes one Shudder.—The reporter calls attention to another block of houses, one of which was a beer saloon. Some of the walls were damp with water that had escaped from the sinks and inundated the floor overhead. He ascended the stairs of another house to examine a sink which one of the female tenants said was "horrible." Situated in the hall, at the head of the first flight of stairs, was found a little dark closet that contained the sink. The guide brought a light to show its internal arrangements, but the atmosphere of the closet was so foul that the candle burned with difficulty. The smell was not to be described. Nick Bottom was not half so puzzled in his effort to describe his dream, says the reporter, as one would be to describe this stench. "It was nauseating, sickening, and disgusting to the last degree, and we shudder as we write at the memory of the offence then and there offered to our sense of sight and smell. It was abominable, and when one of the tenants averred it had made her sick, the wonder was that she had not died."

Miasmatic Scum and Poison.—Leaving the "domestic abominations" described above, the reporter proceeded to the rear yards, which had become the receptacle of all manner of filth and kitchen offal. "Pools of water," he says, "covered with a green and miasmatic scum, stood festering in the yards, exhaling poison, and making the neighborhood a nuisance. The privies were the *ultima Thule* of offensiveness. They had been used in common by the inhabitants of these domiciliary fever-breeders until they had become unusable. Their condition accounted for the fact that the cellars were little better than cess-pools ; and the tenant said that pits had been dug in the yards to receive the contents of the privy vaults. The yards and areas to these houses, and the houses themselves, from the cellar to the roof, were unmitigably filthy. Every step seemed to disclose some new stench, and every glance of the eye discovered some fresh abomination. No words can do justice to such sights and smells, while the depth of degredation and moral uncleanness to which such external filth must necessarily lead is a subject for the courts and the missionary societies."

DISEASE INEVITABLE.—In reference to the fearful atmospheric abominations, which have just been described so vividly, the reporter truthfully says, "Disease is inevitable to all who habitually eat, drink, or breathe putrescence, and death the only result that can reasonably be expected when some virulent poison daily and hourly assails the human system. The vitality which resists the attack of to-day, sinks powerless beneath the assaults of to-morrow."

FILTH AND GARBAGE.—Still another block of houses came under the reporter's notice, of which he speaks as follows: "The filth and garbage within and about the premises became daily more putrid, decomposition more rapid, the stench more profound, and the general condition of the houses more abominable. A corps of men removed at least four cart-loads of putrid filth from four of the cellars. A portion of this had to be carried out in buckets on account of its fluidity. During this process, one of the men, overpowered by the stench, became sick, and was compelled to leave the work. As the block consists of nine houses, some conception may be formed of the habits of the tenants, the carelessness of the lessee, and the amount of the accumulations of refuse matter."

ROTTEN ROW.—This is the name of a place in Greenwich Street, above Canal Street. By any other name the reporter thinks it would smell as sweet, but by no other name could it be so well described. The several buildings which come under this designation swarm with tenantry. There are places in this Row where the fresh air and bright sunlight never come. There was a cellar, for instance, which had neither inlet nor outlet, excepting the door which shut level with the pavement. Within this enclosure a woman was sewing by the dim light, while two children were playing about the place. The good woman received the reporter pleasantly, and gave some account of her domestic affairs. When she leaves home to work she shuts the door, locks the youngsters in, and has the satisfaction of knowing that she will find them there when she comes home. For this miserable habitation the poor woman paid six dollars per month.

PRESENT ASPECT OF TENEMENT HOUSES, SEPTEMBER, 1869.--The report of the Board of Health in relation to tenement-houses, made September 8, 1869, and published in the *Tribune*, September 9th, does not indicate any improvement in these houses. The report says:

The poor are crowded into small, unlighted, and unventilated rooms, and, with few or no conveniences for cleanliness, domestic filth in its worst forms accumulates within and around their homes. Living under such conditions year after year, the tenant-house population creates an atmosphere charged with the elements of the most virulent and destructive diseases. Infantile life is scarcely prolonged through the first year. The decimated generations which arrive at adult years, exhibit the feebleness and decrepitude of age. It is among this class that all forms of contagious disease thrive as in a congenial soil, and from it that they so frequently burst forth and spread through the neighboring communities. And every year, whatever may be the general healthfulness of the town, it is in the tenement-house districts that the great balance-sheet of its excessive mortality is made up. In New York City the tenement-house system presents its worst features. More than one-half of the total population live in tenement houses. The great majority of these houses are old buildings, reconstructed for the purpose of packing the poor away, on the plan of the largest number in the smallest space. From 80 to 120 people to a superficial area of 25x100 feet may be regarded as the rule rather than the exception.

The report goes on to say that the worst class of tenement-houses, found by the examining committee, were those where a landlord had accommodations for ten families and upward; and these buildings comprise more than half of the tenement-houses of the city, and accommodate fully two-thirds of the entire tenement-house population. The report proceeds as follows:

The little colony exhibit in their rooms and in the areas around their dwellings extreme want of care. The street in front of the place was reeking with slops and garbage; the alleys and passage-ways were foul with excrements; the court was imperfectly paved, wet, and covered with domestic refuse; the privies, located in a close court between the rear and front houses, were dilapidated, and gave out volumes of noisome odors which filled the whole area, and were diffused through all the rooms opening upon it; and the halls and apartments of the wretched occupants were close, unventilated, and unclean. The complaint was universal among the tenants that they are entirely uncared for, and that the only answer to their request to have the place put in order by repairs and necessary improvements is, that they must pay their rent or leave. Inquiry will disclose the fact that the owner of the property is a wealthy gentleman or lady, either living in an aristocratic part of the city, or in a neighboring city, or, as was occasionally found to be the case, in Europe.

Inspector James makes the annexed report:

" During the past three years it has been my duty to pay frequent visits to tenement-houses Nos. 433 and 435 West Thirty Ninth Street, for the purpose of investigating the complaint of some citizen regarding their sanitary condition,

and have, without exception, found the premises filthy, almost beyond description. Each of these houses is a five story building, containing respectively
eighteen and twenty families, whose social and moral condition seems to har-
monize with the appearance of the houses and their surroundings. The halls,
stairways, wall, and ceilings are filthy with dirt and grease; the cellars receive
daily the cast off articles of dress and other refuse matter of the various occupants of the houses; the privies are constantly getting out of order, the sewer
drain obstructed, the vault filled to overflowing, and the floors and seats of the
privy buildings filthy with human excrements to such an extent as to make them
unfit for use, rendering it necessary for the tenants to bring out their excrements
in vessels, to be deposited in the privy vault, by which means the structures
become daily more filthy; the yards are often filthy with garbage and night-soil,
the hydrant drain frequently obstructed, and the hydrant sink overflowing with
filthy water."

THE PEABODY TENEMENT-HOUSES IN LONDON.

In contrast with the miserable and filthy New York tenement-houses, we turn with pleasure to a brief contemplation
of those established in London through the munificence of
Mr. George Peabody, whose death, while we are writing, is
announced by the cable telegraph. The premises at Isling-
ton, as described in a letter from London, consist of four
blocks of buildings, comprising in all 155 tenements, accommodating 650 persons, or nearly 200 families. The whole
cost of these buildings, exclusive of the sum paid for the
land, amounted to £31,690. The principle and organization
in each of these extensive structures is the same. Drainage
and ventilation have been insured with the utmost possible
care, the instant removal of dust and refuse is effected by
means of shafts which descend from every corridor to cellars in
the basement, whence it is carted away; the passages are all
kept clean, and lighted with gas, without any cost to the
tenants; water from cisterns in the roof is distributed by
pipes into every tenement, and there are baths free for all
who desire to use them. Laundries, with wringing-ma-
chines and drying-lofts, are at the service of every inmate,
who is thus relieved from the inconvenience of damp vapors
in their apartments, and the consequent damage to their
furniture and bedding. Every living-room or kitchen is
abundantly provided with cupboards, shelving, and other
conveniences, and each fireplace includes a boiler and an
oven. But what gratifies the tenants, perhaps, more than
any other part of the arrangements, are the ample and airy
spaces which serve as playgrounds for their children, where

The impure air in the school-rooms in New York City and Brooklyn have long been proverbial; but it has not been generally known, so far as I know, that it has tended to shorten the lives of the teachers. A startling fact in relation to this matter has been communicated to me by John Hayes, Esq., a well-known legal gentleman, who was a member of the Board of Education in New York City, and of course well posted in every thing pertaining to our schools. He tells me that the teachers, particularly the women, usually die of consumption in six or seven years. This mortality Mr. Hayes attributes to the impure air of the school-rooms. This is a frightful mortality, and if teachers suffer in this way, the children under their tuition must also suffer. We are surely not justifiable in permitting such a sacrifice of human life, when we can so easily prevent it by proper ventilation, which would cost but a trifling comparative sum. We literally slaughter our children— whom we love so well, and who cling to us for protection and support—by sending them to the public schools. Of what avail is an education if we poison and destroy the body? With regard to consumption, spoken of by Mr. Hayes, we are now told by the medical profession that it is frequently produced by foul air. No wonder, therefore, that school-teachers die so frequently of the disease.

There is no more difficulty in ventilating public school rooms (by the proper method) than other rooms. The worst school in Boston was ventilated by us seven years ago—eight large class rooms with some 500 pupils from the tenement-house population. Prof. Ripley Nichols and Dr. Draper measured the air exhausted with their anemometer, finding and officially reporting exactly the volume of air I had contracted to give, and which my own anemometer also had shown, i. e. 20 cubic feet per minute for every scholar, and the atmosphere constantly swept clean of their odors. Some of the more celebrated private schools in New York have also been most satisfactorily treated by us; but the public schools continue to be a disgrace, a nuisance and a scandal, for foul air and mortality among the children.

As to the course of the Board of Education in New York City, on the subject of Ventilation, it would hardly be possible to write too severely. It cannot be pretended that the school rooms are ventilated. Nor can it be pretended that there is any difficulty in ventilating them. Not even the ignorance of the Board, in regard to the proper means of ventilation can be pleaded in excuse. There are ways that might be tried, at least, (if there were a disposition to do anything,) besides the frivolous contrivances, utterly useless, that ornament the buildings erected under their authority, where in any case a pretense of ventilation is attempted. The Board of Education to-day, whatever may be the worth and respectability of its members proper, is practically run by the same official *factotums* as for the last fifteen or twenty years, and in the same way. It is absolutely amazing that a body of gentlemen of so much character, after consenting to assume the high responsibility of Commissioners of Education for a city like this, can allow a permanent set of ignorant and indifferent official servitors to take their duty off their hands in so vital a matter as the ventilation of the public schools. If they cannot afford to give their valuable time to such details, they ought at least to know the deplorable state of their crowded schoolrooms, and to commit the remedy to some one who knows something and cares something about it. It is easy to show, and this very book gives them the means of ascertaining the fact, that every schoolroom in the city can be ventilated in such a manner as to leave no impurities offensive to the most critical senses, or discoverable by scientific tests, in the fullest school or in the thickest weather; and that without exposing a single individual to the hurtful influence of draughts. If the Board of Education, or any body else, will take the trouble to examine into the facts, it will be found that the air of schoolrooms and churches, and in short all sorts of places, can be changed at any prescribed rate per minute, whether it be 50 or 500 or 5,000 cubic feet, and the air taken out from any and all parts of the room BY MEASURE as exact and uniform as the measurement of grain by an elevator, or the flow of gas through a meter.

THE FOULEST SCHOOL-HOUSE IN NEW YORK.—Oliver
Dyer has told us about the "Wickedest Man in New York,"
and it falls to our lot to say something about the *Foulest
School-House in New York*. The School referred to is in
City Hall Place, not far from the Five Points—a fitting and
suggestive companionship. The story is this: Mr. Jackson,
Chairman of the Warming and Ventilating Committee under
the old Board of Education, consulted us in reference to the
ventilation of the schools. I requested him to send me to
the foulest school-house in the city, as a test of my ability
to ventilate it, and this one was selected for the purpose.

I decided to make the experiment, and proceeded to
examine the building, accompanied by my draughtsman.
The school was in session. We passed through twenty or
more of the rooms. Each room was crowded with boys and
girls. There were probably 1,500 pupils in the aggregate. The atmosphere was horrible beyond description. No
words can give an adequate idea of the combination of
stenches that saluted our unwilling nostrils. My draughtsman became deathly sick, and had to leave the rooms on
three different occasions in pursuit of fresh air.

When we reached the lower floor of the building, the
female principal invited our attention to a particular room,
which we all entered. The stench in this enclosure was
almost beyond human endurance. "This room," said the
lady, "we call the *hospital*." "Why do you call it the
hospital?" we inquired. "Because," she answered, "no
female teacher, during the last year and a half, has been
able to teach here more than six days without becoming
sick."

I furnished a plan to Mr. Jackson for the ventilation of
this very foul place—this nest of free-school abominations—
and agreed to perform my work successfully or make no
charge for my labors. Before my proposition was acted
upon, however, there was a change in the Board of Education, and thus the matter has rested ever since.

WRETCHED CONDITION OF THE SCHOOL-HOUSES OF THE ME-
TROPOLIS—THE KILLING OF TEACHERS AND PUPILS BY
FOUL AIR.

Under this heading the *New York Tribune* for July 27,
1867, has a report in reference to the Public Schools of our
metropolis, which occupies rather more than four columns.
Its revelations are of the most frightful character. We invite attention to the report, so that the Board of Education
may be constantly reminded of the duty which they owe
the public. The *Tribune*, referring to the report, expresses
itself as follows :

The facts which our reporters tell in other columns, concerning the sanitary
condition of the school-houses of this city, will shake the popular confidence.
Thorough inspection of a large proportion of our public schools, located in
widely separated portions of the city, shows that not one single building can be
found wherein the occupants have not been daily poisoned with foul air, through
utter want of any adequate system of ventilation. Sixty, eighty, or one hundred
children have been packed into rooms capable of decently accommodating only
one-half that number, and then compelled to breathe the vitiated air which finds
no way of escape from the over-crowded room. In some cases attempts have
been made to provide a way for the fresh air to get in, or for the foul air to get
out, but the architects of these devices have not realized the importance of
combining the two movements. In most of the school-houses the windows are
depended upon for a supply of fresh air, but on damp or cold days it is manifestly unsafe to have the draft from the windows precipitated directly upon the
heads and backs of those pupils who, by the faulty construction of the assembly
or recitation rooms, are placed upon a level with the window sills. In these
vital points the more recently constructed school edifices are no better than the
old ones. Money has been lavishly expended upon some of these houses, but
not a dollar devoted to that which should be insured to every individual when he
or she enters any public institution—pure air. If the question of cost is brought
up as an objection to remedying the evil which now exists in these houses, it
should be a sufficient reply to say that the health and perhaps the lives of two
thousand teachers and two hundred thousand children are dependant upon a
reform.

Let us now follow the reporter of the *Tribune* in his
visits to the schools. Out of 150 buildings, he examined only twenty-one, and says, "Although confident we
have seen the best, we are by no means certain of having seen
the worst. The best are bad enough. They tell us a sufficiently harrowing story." The reporter further says, "Bad
as are places of worship and amusement, our public schools
are worse. How bad they are we never knew until we beheld
what the readers of the *Tribune* may now see by looking
through an unprejudiced pair of spectacles."

GRAMMAR SCHOOL No. 33.—This was the first school visited by the reporter. In describing it he speaks of the "hermetically sealed galleries" as having "an insupportable atmosphere," and goes on with his description as follows :

" Does not this bad air affect you ?" was asked of a teacher whose pale face interested us.

" Of course it does. We very often have headaches, and teachers never have good blood." Later we saw this young girl in a small recitation room, surrounded by eighty children, who were divided into two classes, she teaching one division, while the assistant beside her taught the other. None of the other recitation rooms were quite as offensive as this extreme case, nevertheless they were all objectionable, and without other than window ventilation. Every one contained twice as many children as there was air for them to breathe. Passing to the Grammar Department, we were ushered into a large and comfortable looking hall, ornamented at one end with scriptural texts, among which was the command, " Love thy neighbor as thyself." It may be satisfactory to the Local Board of that Ward to know that it strengthened us in our determination to play the ungrateful part of public inspector and benefactor. There was nothing to complain of in this hall, save that, as usual, no adequate provision had been made for ventilation. " How do you ventilate?" was asked. " By means of windows. Those two ventilators are almost useless.

* * * * * * * * * *

Going down into the play-ground we found that the yard room was exceedingly small, and that the most of the recess is spent in the basement of the building, which, being open on one side, is called a covered yard. The ceiling is low, no sun ever penetrates within, and the atmosphere was much worse than any we had yet passed through. Hundreds of children stood about and inhaled stagnant carbonic acid gas at every breath. Instead of bracing the lungs to endure the bad air of recitation-rooms, recess aggravates rather than diminishes the evil. This statement holds good for many other schools. Nauseated, we made our way across the yard to a primary section, which, owing to the overcrowded condition of the school-building, had taken refuge in the basement of an adjoining church. This basement is several feet under ground, is always damp, even in the warmest weather—on the 12th day of June there was a fire in the stove—and for darkness, abominable ventilation and general unhealthiness, has not its equal outside of a tenement house. In winter the rain took possession of the floor, until a hole was made near the door, whereby the invading element now descends into the cellar and adds to the perpetual dampness. And this basement, for which an annual rent of $800 is paid, has been occupied during the last three or four years. Complaints have been made to the Board of Education, who have referred them to a committee, and there the matter has ended. That such a scandal should be tolerated is a marvel, and were not the children of this Ward of poor parentage, the fact would long since have been made public. Because children are wretchedly accommodated at home, however, is no reason why they should obtain nothing better at school, and to subject educated teachers to such a pestilent prison, is adding insult to injury.

GRAMMAR SCHOOL No. 17.—Rebuilt, says the reporter, in 1859. A marble slab was conspicuous, containing the names of the Commissioners, architect, etc. There being an architect in the case, the reporter naturally inquired how the building was ventilated. "By opening the windows," was the answer. The heat also was unequally distributed, so that the pupils near the stove were baked, while those at a distance suffered with the cold. This was particularly the case in the galleries, where all the light and air came from one window immediately behind the highest bench. When the window was open, the children on the upper benches would freeze; when closed, the atmosphere was impregnated with poison. The balance of the story is related as follows:

Descending to the Primary Department, we found matters worse, instead of better. This portion of the school is always more fully attended than any other, and as the building in Forty-Seventh Street has 3,000 registered pupils, it requires no vivid imagination to picture the child-packing of the basement floor. This I call the Black Hole of Calcutta. said a teacher showing us a dark gallery. It was a pitiful sight to see all those helpless little children being drilled in disease rather than in spelling. Crossing a miserably confined play-ground, we entered a neglected looking building which, originally a third-rate private house, had been converted into school-rooms. It is almost needless to say that the rooms—and there are six—are small, with low ceilings, and in every respect worse than any in the school proper, galleries excepted. Every room was crowded with little boys, and every room was insufferable in point of atmosphere. It is but just to add that this state of things will not last much longer, as a new school-house in Fifty-second street will be opened next season. This additional accommodation will do away with the necessity for a supplementary building; but as the evil has been tolerated for six years, it is rather important to bring it before the public. The children are of excellent parentage, and evidently accustomed to decent homes. The wrong done them, therefore, is the greater, as by attending school their condition is made worse instead of better. That they are sent into such an atmosphere shows the culpable neglect of parents, who rarely, if ever, visit the schools where their children pass 30 hours of every week. Bidding farewell to the "dreary pile," we wondered how the architect could have screwed his courage to the sticking place of a permanent marble slab, that now looked to me more like a grave-stone, on which might well have been inscribed, " Sacred to the Perpetuity of Carbonic Acid Gas."

GRAMMAR SCHOOL No. 40.—This building, although erected but three years ago, is represented by the reporter as being more imperfectly ventilated than any yet visited. The upper hall is capable of seating 800 boys, and is hermetically sealed, excepting the windows. The same is true of the small rooms on the same floor. Below, the rear recitation rooms are most uncomfortable. In two of these, which are so small and stifling as to be almost uninhabitable, an experimental ventilation is being tried. Whether the air is any better than it was, the reporter does not know.

It is now quite bad enough; yet classes of fifty recite in these hen-coops. Owing to a high wall, several of the rooms are very dark, so dark in winter as to render the ciphering on the blackboard a difficult operation. The reporter completes the picture of the above school as follows:

Several teachers in the Grammar Department complained of the bad air and absence of light. The stench in the playground is unparalleled in our investigation, for added to the gases from the outbuildings are those proceeding from a large stable in Twenty-fourth street, in the rear of which this school-house was deliberately built. We are also told that the ground on which it stands was formerly occupied by a slaughter-house. Perhaps it would do no harm were the Board of Health to concern itself in our educational establishments, and sit in judgment upon the purchases of school property. Children will not complain, for it is astonishing with what facility their lungs accommodate themselves to foul gases.

GRAMMAR SCHOOL No. 50.—The building devoted to this school is on high ground, with no nuisance in the neighborhood, and no high walls to obstruct either light or air. The play-ground was clean and fresh, and there was no perceptible odor from the out-buildings. Thus far the reporter is complimentary, but he says the building is without adequate ventilation. Windows, as usual, are chiefly relied on for that purpose. He says there are a few "upper ventilators" in the Primary Department, but acknowledges that they render very little service. An "upper ventilator" is understood to be merely a register.

PRIMARY SCHOOL No. 29.—This building is dirty and without ventilation. "The play-ground is said to be damp, and the four recitation-rooms on the same floor are equally so, added to which two of them are quite dark. Yet, in spite of dampness and darkness, seventy-two boys are huddled into a space of about 10 by 15 feet; and in a somewhat larger room, one hundred boys clad in quite as much dirt as clothing, are packed as closely as herrings. The teacher in attendance complained very seriously of the atmosphere, and if offensive with open doors and windows, what must be the condition of such a room in winter? Much of the evil wrought is owing to receiving more children than the school can accommodate, one thousand being the number registered, and six hundred being the maximum for comfort and health."

PRIMARY SCHOOL No. 38.—With regard to ventilation in this building, an intelligent teacher said, "We depend entirely upon the windows." But what do you do in the winter? The teacher answered, "Windows still, and then the platform is so cold that I nearly freeze. I take refuge in the class-rooms."

In one of the class-rooms, says the reporter, the air is so bad, owing to the vicinity of a water-closet belonging to a public school in the rear, that the health of the teacher who formerly occupied it failed signally.

GRAMMAR SCHOOL No. 1.—This does not seem to be a No. 1 school so far as heat and ventilation are concerned. This is the reporter's story :

Entering the Girls' Grammar Department, we discovered a few vacuum but no plenum ventilators. "Windows are our salvation" said a teacher who ushered us into two small air-tight class-rooms, in each of which sat 50 scholars. During the winter one corner is rendered so hot, in consequence of the furnace flue passing up between the walls, that no one can sit in its vicinity, while at a short distance from it the room is quite cold. This department has 50 more pupils than can be properly accommodated.

One of the female principals said to the reporter, " You are right in finding fault with the ventilation, but in the Primary Department you will find it much worse. I was down there fifteen minutes yesterday, and felt that I had remained fifteen minutes too long."

The reporter adds, "This teacher was correct Five hundred and fifty little children are herded together in a space only large enough for two-thirds the number, and the two galleries are not only damp and dark, but in winter are very cold, a condition of temperature that precludes the opening of windows. As whatever ventilation there may be comes from below only, the state of these galleries must be poisonous indeed, especially as 150 children are congregated in each gallery from 9 o'clock a.m. to 2 o'clock p.m. Even with doors and windows open, the teacher confined there shook her head mournfully, and told a sad story of an assistant who had been obliged to obtain a month's leave of absence after doing duty in this human shamble."

PRIMARY SCHOOL No. 8.—Erected in 1857. Would be creditable to New York, says the reporter, had efficient ventilation been procured. "There are egress ventilators productive of little good. The air in some of the upper class-rooms is close, and several teachers bewailed the fact.

The covered play-ground teems with foul gases, and the area open to the sun is about the width of an ally-way. Six hundred and fifty children seek recreation here."

PRIMARY SCHOOL No. 42.—In the Primary Department the reporter found 1,100 children where 500 ought to be. "How do you manage?" the reporter asked. "Well, we almost hang the children up," was the answer.

PRIMARY SCHOOL No. 1.—Situated at 105 Ludlow Street. One of the most ancient and discreditable school-buildings in the city. On the ground floor is an unventilated, low, and dingy assembly room, where 280 children, divided into three classes, recite simultaneously. Back of this are smaller rooms, equally objectionable, one having only one window, which window is a poor apology for the same, being obstructed by a staircase. On the story above, the air and arrangements are better, yet so crowded are the rooms that we saw one little girl perched on the stove.

"Does that little girl sit on the stove in winter?" asked the reporter.

"Oh, no, then she stands up."

GRAMMER SCHOOL No. 15.—This is an old building which has been re-modeled at an expense of $70,000, but without any arrangements for ventilation.

"Your class-rooms must be very unhealthly," said the reporter to the Principal of the Boy's Grammer Department.

"Yes," he replied ; "this room was formerly so suffocating that I made strenuous efforts to abate the discomfort. It required six months' complaining to get a window cut through into the assembly room, and this I only succeeded in by shutting a trustee up in a room and desiring him to remain there five minutes. When he came out he promised that the window should be cut, and it was cut."

"By this device," say the reporter, "the foul air of the class-room escapes into the general assembly-room, instead of an external outlet."

"In the Primary Department," continues the reporter, "the want of ventilation was still more apparent, and descending to the basement we were shown four class-rooms that are unfit for occupation, owing to the dampness caused by the made-land on which the school is built. It rests on piles. Yet two years ago the basement play-ground was occupied by the Primary Department. One foot under ground, low, and unventilated, with windows so near the floor that when open the air blew directly on the children, this cellar was a disgrace to humanity. One teacher died of consumption contracted here, and it is not doubted that many children have been borne to early graves as a reward for a regular attendance at Grammar School No. 15."

GRAMMAR SCHOOL No. 47.—This school is in a good location, and receives a fine class of pupils. The building nevertheless is represented as signally deficient in all sanitary requirements. It is furnished with what is called "egress ventilators," which the reporter thinks ought to be abolished, as the air within the building is the worst that can be imagined. Hearing many complaints against the school, the reporter asked a teacher what was her proportion of absentees on account of sickness. She answered, "Fourteen out of forty, and I am often obliged to excuse girls on account of headache caused by the bad air of the class-rooms. Our only means of ventilation is by the windows, so that in winter it is a choice between catching cold and inhaling poison. The girls generally prefer the poison. Nor can we always obtain pure air by opening the windows, as the odors from the out-buildings are sometimes very bad." In addition to the information thus elicited, the reporter says, "We ourselves can testify to the abominable atmosphere of the assembly-rooms when filled with girls. Again, all the light from these rooms proceeds from windows facing the desks, an arrangement which is fatal to the eyesight of hundreds of girls."

PART II.

WHAT IS, AND WHAT IS NOT, VENTILATION.

CHARACTERISTICS OF GOUGE'S SYSTEM.

I. Our Distinctive Proposal is not, simply to put up certain ventilating apparatus, nor to introduce such flues, &c., as, according to the philosophy of heat and gases, ought, theoretically, to create the desired movement of air; nor merely to remove, in a general way, such impurity or closeness of air as may be noticed by the senses. All such things as these are matters of opinion and doubt, and the most favorable estimation of them can be but indefinite. On the contrary, the definite, tangible thing we in all cases contract to do, and about which there can be no mistake or dispute, is to exhaust (and replace) any prescribed volume of air per minute, whether 50 or 5000 cubic feet, at the outlet of each room; replacing the same continuously with the like quantity of fresh air, warm or cool to suit the season; and delivering the result by measure as indisputable as that of the yard-stick or bushel. This, and this alone, is is what WE mean by Ventilation.

We assume this to be the only thing that will satisfy an intelligent and practical demand for ventilation at the present day, in view of the notorious failure of theoretical plans, and of the insufficiency of the "nose test" for impurities, particularly carbonic acid—viz: a sufficient, stipulated and measured quantity of fresh air every minute in exchange for as much vitiated air removed; and this is what we undertake to deliver at all seasons, regardless of the state of weather or atmosphere, exactly as a grain merchant contracts to deliver so many thousand bushels of wheat.

We think we act advisedly in setting down the above among the peculiar characteristics of Gouge's Ventilation.

If parties who offer an indefinite something which they are pleased to call ventilation, at one half to one tenth of our price, would agree to deliver fresh air as we do, in measured quantities, charging only for what they (uniformly) deliver, vast sums of money now wasted would be saved to owners, the test of value would be infallible and evasion impossible, and we should not be obliged to tax the confidence of the public with the strange fact that ventilation, (in the only sense we consider genuine,) is not so much as pretended outside of Gouge's method.

II. We handle air as a material substance, having weight, inertia, &c., and requiring a constant force, like any other substance, to keep it moving in any one direction. Consequently we do *not* rely on accidental differences of gravity between inside and outside atmosphere, to cause the former to ascend and escape; whereas it is perhaps as often liable to balance the other way and descend, and for a great part of the time the weight is so nearly equal as to produce hardly perceptible motion either way. Nor, again, even in the season of fires, do we offer the ascensional force of a pipe-full of warmed air as an adequate motor for the removal of hundreds of cubic feet per minute from a room. Experience, if not philosophy, has proved that nothing less, in the way of simple heat, than a steam-boiler furnace in full action, can maintain at all times the suction necessary for removing a considerable volume of air per minute. This, of course, is expensive, and impracticable in ordinary cases.

What, then, is our motive power?

It is furnished by an ordinary argand gas burner, operating through a peculiar form of flue, so constructed as to use the well known velocity of flame, as an INDUCTIVE power, entraining through precisely adjusted orifices, copious currents of air; such as are perceived when a flame is started with paper, straw or shavings, at the draft throat of any well-constructed chimney or stove. The peculiar discovery which lies at the bottom of our system is the wonderful capacity of a small flame to entrain copious and rapid currents of air, through the special adjustments of compression, induction and expansion, invented by Mr. Gouge. No less than fifteen years were spent by him in perfecting the adaptations, proportions, &c., that now enable us to construct a ventilating system certain to exhaust and replace the exact volume of air per minute required, in any room or any building, large or small. It is most remarkable that the draft power developed by a small flame, through the apparatus invented by Mr. Gouge, increases with every induction orifice opened, so far as we have had occasion to carry the experiment in ventilating large office buildings. There is nothing theoretical about this. The fact was never theoretically discovered. But it can now be verified by any person with his own breath, by means of an instrument to be found in the philosophical apparatus of certain schools: a miniature flue on the Gouge principle, in detachable joints, the addition of each of which, with its additional inlet, is found to multiply many fold the force of the blast from the mouth as it issues at the extreme end.

In the absence of gas, an ordinary (argand) oil burner answers the purpose in our ventilators. In any case, the ascending current once established requires but a small expenditure of gas, from one to three cubic feet per hour, to sustain it with its tributaries in lively action all the year around.

III. The fact last noted—perhaps the hardest to believe without ocular demonstration, which however can be had by anybody wishing to inquire, in hundreds of places—brings us to our third characteristic, viz.: that the first cost of the apparatus is also substantially the last. Ample, uniform and certain ventilation goes on thenceforward through day and night, at a nominal cost for gas. The most vexatious and fruitless, yet common, of all expenses—that of putting in and turning out again, one after another, a succession of useless ventilating contrivances—is stopped or prevented, and the same demonstrated, from the moment of setting our apparatus in motion.

IV. An adequate suction, by which the whole movement of air from and into the apartment is sustained, is one of the essential characteristics of true ventilation. You may *drive* a great deal of fresh air through a room without removing what there was there before. But a vigorous suction, located at the proper points, must draw equally from all directions, and from every corner, crack and cranny, and is the only effectual means of a thorough cleansing and constant change of air.

V. Prices cannot be given in general terms and rules. It is necessary to make a personal survey, and to draw a well-considered plan for the most effective application of the system to the premises, before an estimate of cost can be made. Rooms must be measured in every direction, their capacity calculated, the number of occupants, lights and fires taken into account, the proper supply of air for each provided by accurate openings and ducts at the right places, the best location for uptake flues, and the best mode of conducting the tributary flues from the several apartments, determined, with all the sizes and proportions and points of expansion in the flues, and many other critical points considered. This is expensive professional work, which cannot be deputed to employees, nor be afforded without a reasonable probability that the estimate will be accepted. All that we promise in general is that our charges for professional time, materials, and workmanship, are uniform, sufficient to pay for the best we can procure, and not exorbitant for the outlay we make and the results we accomplish.

It may be well, also, in this connection, to caution parties that the hints and principles here thrown out cannot be applied to practice by amateurs or novices, with the *smallest* degree of success. There is no rule, system or formula extant, by which the peculiar result known as Gouge's Ventilation has been worked out by others. Those wishing ventilation can easily satisfy themselves by examination of buildings ventilated by us, whether we do the thing we contract to do or not; also, what other parties, if any, propose to risk their own money exclusively, on the uniform delivery and removal of stipulated volumes of air, by measure, by means of only a small gas jet. If convenient, they might also profitably inspect the operation (or non-operation) of one or two attempted imitations of our methods. The genuine work of ventilation done by us for the last twenty-five years will speak for itself in all cases; of which we can refer to thousands, including every conceivable kind of place requiring ventilation, such as banks, insurance and office buildings, private houses, churches, schools, public halls, hotels, stables, ice closets, &c., &c.

VENTILATED ICE CLOSETS AND REFRIGERATORS.

The necessity of thorough ventilation for preserving food in a wholesome state is, if possible, still less appreciated than its necessity for the well-being of human and animal life. Cold temperature, without fresh air, only retards decay to a slow and subtile process that may be called *staling*, and that makes the food practically more harmful than if spoiled entirely, since in the latter case nobody would eat it. On the other hand, abundance of fresh air will preserve food in better condition without ice, than it can be kept in ice without fresh air. The imperishability of meat hung in the pure atmosphere of the Colorado Parks, &c., illustrates this point.

Few are aware of the further fact that a constant change of fresh air will preserve *ice* longer than confined air, and therefore a positively ventilated refrigerator will require *less ice* for a given temperature. Although the fresh air comes in warm, its active vaporization of moisture absorbs more heat than it introduces. In simply melting the ice, but 143 degrees of heat are absorbed; but in the further process of vaporizing the water, by the agency of fresh air, 824 degrees further are got rid of; much more than compensating for the warmth of the fresh air, as all experience with our ice closets demonstrates. A positive ventilating current, just sufficient to carry off all the free moisture practicable, would be the ideal of an ice preserver as well as meat preserver. Gouge's method of ventilation does in practice preserve both ice and food longer, as well as in better condition, than any mere enclosure ever devised for excluding air and warmth. For this purpose, as in all effective ventilation, some steady and adequate force is indispensable, and the best and cheapest is the same that we employ in ventilating buildings. A good preserving closet will, to be sure, cost something. That of the Fifth Avenue Hotel, where they hang all their beef a fortnight to perfect its juices, before sending it to the kitchen, cost $4000, and the proprietor has often said he would not do without it for $100,000. But in any large establishment such a closet (on the proper scale of cost) will pay directly the best return of all the rooms in the house. With any family who can afford the luxury of absolute freshness in all their perishable marketing, the cost will be remembered only with the pleasure of money well spent.

VENTILATION *vs.* NON-VENTILATION OF PRODUCE CARS.

For the purpose of reducing to figures the thermal conditions affecting grain and perishable produce in transit to the seaboard, we have obtained from the meteorological records the average temperature at principal points on the middle trunk lines for a number of years past, the mean of which may be assumed to represent, roughly, the average temperature through which a car will pass on its way East from the great forwarding centres :

	June.	July.	Aug.	3 mos.
Boston	66 deg.	72 deg.	69 deg.	69 deg.
New York	68 "	73 "	73 "	71½ "
Albany	68 "	72 "	70 "	70 "
Pittsburg	69 "	73 "	71 "	71 "
Cincinnati	71 "	76 "	74 "	73¾ "
Milwaukee	65 "	70 "	67 "	67¼ "
Chicago	63 "	71 "	68 "	67¼ "
Average temperature	67 "	72 "	70 "	69¼ "

We may take, then, the round figure of 70° as a maximum for the average heat of the atmosphere outside the car. The cumulative heat in the material of the car from direct sunshine will raise the temperature of the interior at least 50 per cent. above that of the atmosphere without, or say to 105°. Any one who has ever stepped into a close car, or garret, on which a summer sun has been shining some hours, can confirm the moderation of this statement without the aid of a thermometer. Any one who has attempted to sleep in quarters similarly situated, in summer, will understand that the cooling by night of a car and contents thus heated through by day, will not equal half the difference outside. The difference outside will not generally exceed, at its extreme, 20°, or a reduction of say 10° in the average. Half as much reduction will be the utmost we can realize on the inside, leaving the average temperature there 100°. A considerable heat of fermentation must also be developed, but a round hundred will answer about as well as more to represent the condition to which freight in ordinary cars is subjected under the summer sun. So far is this from exaggeration, we are informed that even in very cool weather of say 40°, the effect of the sun on such cars is so great that butter cannot be carried in them without spoiling.

Now, suppose that the atmospheric pressure against the car in motion at twelve miles per hour were utilized, so as to scour out the heated air and exhalations from every corner and crevice of the car and its load, and replace them with fresh air from outside, in effect creating a constant movement of pure, dry, temperate air throughout all the interstices of the grain or other produce. Let it be remembered that this pure and cooling flow throughout the mass takes the place of a stagnant atmosphere, heated to 100°, and saturated with exhalations of organic matter until it can hold no more and precipitates the accumulating excess on all the surfaces of the produce in an unctuous and putrefying sweat—putrefaction that may indeed be retarded and kept below the temperature of volatilization (or offensive odor) by half filling the car with ice; but which cannot be wholly stopped, short of freezing, nor balked of its sure development at last, whenever bulk is broken.

On the other hand, consider the opposite part these moist exhalations are compelled to act when subjected to the through flow of pure, dry, active air. They become as useful as they were otherwise detrimental, by occasioning a further and important reduction of temperature by evaporation, which brings it materially below the average outside. This has been very pointedly shown by experiment in a passenger car, where the external air pressure resulting from motion was drawn through the interior, in a hot day in 1876, by a Gouge ventilator, on the Pennsylvania Railroad. Temperature was taken with everything thrown open, so as to identify perfectly the interior and exterior atmosphere. Then everything was closed except the pressure ducts, to see what would be their proper effect alone. One would naturally expect a rise of the mercury from thus closing up a car full of passengers in a hot day. The effect, however, was the reverse. The mercury shortly began to fall, until it remained at nearly three degrees lower than with all open. The volume of air changed may or may not have been greater, but its current being narrowed to inlet and exhaust passages adapted to give it greater velocity, increased the activity of its diffusion by the distributing orifices. And the effect of this more actively distributed ventilation in lowering the mercury, could be accounted for in no other way than by the fanning it gave to the only moist surfaces in the case—

those of the passengers. In other words, the increased evaporation that so sensibly cools a person (or other moist surface) passed over by a current of air, was proved to have absorbed from the air itself the greater portion of the heat thus rendered latent. In fact it evidently could not be otherwise. The tendency of every particle of pure air touching a particle of water is to instantly suck it up in vapor, and in vaporizing it renders latent the enormous amount of 967° of heat. This must come, in the main, directly from the air, and the cooling experienced by the surface fanned must result mainly from imparting its own heat in turn to the cooled air in contact; while the comfort of a person so affected would be still further increased by a freer excretion from the skin. When such surfaces are those of very warm passengers, as in the experiment, the net cooling of the air by evaporation must be considerably less than if an equal amount of cool moisture had been vaporized from cool surfaces like those of fresh beef, grain, etc. Hence it would be safe to set down the loss of heat by evaporation in an actively ventilated car filled with moist but not living freight, as at least 5°, and the average summer day temperature of such freight in transit between the Western shipper and the Eastern receiver as not more than 65°.

Of the effect of such a constant absorption and sweeping out of moisture and exhalations by an all-pervading flow of fresh air at such a temperature, it is hardly necessary to reiterate that fermentation, heating, decay, or any kind of deterioration in quality, would be absolutely impossible. Damp grain, instead of perishing in transit, would be cured, and come out "prime" in New York. Dressed meats, fruits and dairy produce would cross the entire continent and Atlantic Ocean as sweet and fresh as they were delivered by the producer at the nearest market town. Lower temperature would never be needed ; yet conceding such necessity, comparatively little ice would be a sufficient auxiliary for any purpose. Positive damage to fresh produce from *too low* a temperature must be guarded against. Receivers and shippers of dairy produce agree that it is safer to transport butter, etc., in an atmosphere of 60° or 65° than a lower one, and better even at 80° than at 40°.

Gouge's Ventilation of Freight and Express Cars for the safe transportation of dressed meats, grain, fruits, vegetables, milk, butter, cheese, eggs, &c., is a tested and acknowledged success, both with and without ice, which needs no other eulogium than the managers of the various Freight, Express and Railroad Companies that have tried it are prepared to give.

In this branch of ventilation, the motion of the train against the resistance of the atmosphere supplies ample motive power for the ventilating current. The inductive and conductive apparatus are adapted to take full advantage of this pressure, distributing it so as to sweep every interstice of the car-load, and to escape as fast as it enters, carrying with it all free moisture, exhalations and impurities, that might initiate fermentation and decay. Grain, which is never otherwise brought from the West to the seaboard, under the most favorable conditions, without deterioration, has been shipped in our cars damp and heated, and instead of spoiling, as it must have done in ordinary cars, has arrived at New York in the dry and perfect condition which it lacked at starting. The gentlemen of the Produce Exchange do not hesitate to say that Gouge's Car Ventilation would insure a higher price for grain, by two or three cents per bushel, above that transported in any way without it. With respect to more perishable produce, it makes transportation profitable where it was before impracticable. Hence, it must in time add largely to the traffic both of railroads and shipping, and increase the distribution of the luxuries of every climate and region among the people of every other.

Our already immense movement of butter and cheese, both to home and foreign markets, will be easily worth one or two cents more per pound when this ventilation becomes universal. In fact, the cumulative heat from the sunshine, in close cars, during more than half the year, requires much more than that value in ice, on on average, to counteract it (which is entirely unnecessary for butter, cheese, &c., in our ventilated cars), while the ice itself, again, incidentally inflicts a certain serious damage on these particular products and some others. Their sound texture and fine flavor can never be repaired after they have once been chilled hard and then transferred to a warm atmosphere.

It is important also, that these self-ventilated preserving cars, while they cost nothing extra for running, dead weight, attendance, repairs, &c., are perfectly adapted for instant service of all sorts, in all directions, and at all seasons, in the general business of a railroad.

OF GOUGE'S SHIP VENTILATION, also, substantially the same facts as the above have been demonstrated by experience. Perishable cargoes of fruit, &c., to and from the West Indies, have been delivered by this means in a condition of perfect soundness, where otherwise they would have been a total loss ; in fact their shipment would not have been attempted

WARMING AND VENTILATING PASSENGER CARS.

VENTILATION AND HEATING BY GOUGE'S SYSTEM, as applied to passenger cars, may be said to reach their perfection. The power is present in abundance, in the movement of the train. It is captured and put to work, in the most effective way for thorough combustion and ventilation. No air can remain in the car long enough to become vitiated ; and none can enter without having been first warmed to a summer temperature, whatever the cold without. There is no difference in the temperature of different parts of the car; the casing of the heater, and the seat next it, being free from uncomfortable warmth, while the remotest seat is equally free from uncomfortable coolness. There is nothing to freeze up or get out of order ; no way to set the car on fire, even by its overturning ; no material addition to dead weight ; a decided economy in fuel ; no loss of space, but, on the contrary, a saving of six sittings in every car, as the apparatus occupies only a single corner, displacing only one double seat ; besides reclaiming four sittings more from the often intolerable heat of the usual stoves.

In the warm season, moreover, the same apparatus affords perfect ventilation, without opening doors and windows to drafts, cinders and dust ; filling the car with pure, fresh, stirring air, several degrees cooler (in ordinary cars it is as much warmer) than that outside in summer weather. The lower temperature here, again, is due to free evaporation, or absorption of moisture as vapor by fresh air ; but the sensible cooling is still greater, because the evaporation takes place at the surface of the person, and the whole loss of heat is thus directly felt ; while the constant change of air prevents any detention of heat in the car.

The following are among the Railroads on which this apparatus is in regular use, in more or less of their cars :—The N. Y. Central & Hudson River ; Delaware, Lackawanna & Western ; Boston & Albany ; Great Western of Canada ; Detroit, Lansing & Northern ; St. Louis and Iron Mountain ; Chicago & Northwestern ; &c.

The following letter from the veteran Superintendent of the Delaware, Lackawanna & Western Railroad, and President of the Sussex Railroad, A. Reasoner, Esq., was written to a director of another railroad company, in reply to a business inquiry concerning the experience of the D.,L. & W. with Gouge's Car Heating & Ventilating Apparatus.

Noting the simple but comprehensive admission of Mr. Reasoner, that our Apparatus *performs all that we claim for it*, (and glancing back at the claims referred to, on the preceding page) the reader will doubtless conclude that this testimony — authoritative, unmasked, and uninfluenced by the motive of courtesy—settles the question of warming and ventilating railway cars, since it is well known that no such results have ever been attained or even claimed by any other apparatus.

DELAWARE, LACKAWANNA & WESTERN R. R. CO.

Sup't's Office, Morris & Essex Division, Hoboken, June 23, 1881.

Samuel Shethar, Esq., 548 Broadway, New York.

Dear Sir:—We have had in use on this road for about three years what is known as the Gouge Warming and Ventilating Apparatus for Passenger Cars.

We first had three Sleeping Cars fitted with them, and I must say I had some doubt as to their practicability, but after a short experience they began to grow in favor, and as we became accustomed to their use found that they performed all that was claimed for them.

This apparatus, in my opinion, possesses many advantages over any other invented for this purpose, and I believe that it will be generally adopted when it becomes better known. The principle is evidently correct, and I think has been thoroughly worked out. It takes but little room, is easy to manage, and is perfectly safe. A large quantity of air enters the car and goes out, without producing drafts. During the past year we have put them on all our new cars, including sleepers, smoking cars, etc., and have found them by far the most satisfactory thing for the purpose which we have ever used.   Yours Respectfully,   A. REASONER, Supt.

THE NEW METHOD OF VENTILATION EXPLAINED—THEORIES CONSIDERED — EXPENSE OF THE GAS — ADAPTATION OF THE VENTILATOR — LEADING POINTS OF THE VENTILA- TOR — PROFESSOR DRAPER'S MODE OF VENTILATION— ADVANTAGES OF THE VENTILATOR.

When we deal with a motive power, and wish to produce practical results, we know that the *cause* must be equal to the *effect*. All systems of ventilation, therefore, which do not recognize an adequate motive power, must be failures; and thus we have had repeated failures in this department of art and science, notwithstanding very plausible and apparently brilliant theories, which, in some instances, have seemed to captivate the judgment of able and distinguished men.

Theories should not be valued in reference to ventilation unless it is shown that they are in correspondence with prac- tical results of an unquestionable and satisfactory character. If a church, kitchen, parlor, stable, banking-house or other place is to be ventilated, the first question should be, Can the foul air be got out, and pure air be made to take its place? If the answer is Yes, and the work is duly accomplished, it will be time enough to look after a theory, or to discuss problems in science and philosophy.

When air is made to ascend through a flue in virtue of a positive irresistible force, which has been created artificially, then, and not till then, shall we have a perfect ventilation ; and this desideratum accomplished, we need not trouble nor vex ourselves about the upward and downward currents of air in chimneys, or other nice theoretical questions or problems.

The motive force to which reference is made above is the one through which our mode of ventilation is always accomplished. It consists of heated currents of air, which ascend through a flue, and by the strong ascensional power which is thus created every vestige of foul air — every unpleasant odor—every atom of the noxious gases—are car- ried irresistibly away and scattered to the four winds.

The air within the ventilator is heated and set in motion by the combustion of gas, kerosene, etc., as already described, (see Description of Cut, opposite title-page,) and it is this device which we have secured by Letters-Patent—

which has enabled us to ventilate so many foul places to the entire satisfaction of our employers. We will assert again, that a jet of gas burning within a flue, properly arranged, has a remarkable power in rarefying the air and producing powerful up-moving currents. Heat communicated to a flue or chimney by a stove, or furnace, external to it, as previously stated, is not to be compared with this in its power of producing ascensional currents, and withal can not be employed so continuously, nor with so little expense, as the jet of gas.

The apparatus, as a whole, with its lantern, flues, etc., constitutes what is termed *"Gouge's Atmospheric Ventilator,"* and, when properly adjusted, will effectually ventilate the dampest cellar or basement, the deepest subterranean vault, or the foulest "black hole" that can be imagined, or brought within the range of its power.

The *expense of the gas* used for ventilating purposes is trifling. Commencing with an ordinary burner, we soon establish a strong up-moving current within the ventilator, which, after a short time, can be maintained by a feeble jet of gas, not amounting to more than one foot per hour. Thus we have an efficient motive power, operating constantly, day and night, without the necessity of any supervision or attendance, producing the most satisfactory ventilation, and furnishing a full supply of fresh air to one's kitchen, stable, sleeping-room, or other apartment.

ADAPTATION OF THE VENTILATOR, ETC.—Simple and obvious as is the principle of ventilation herein set forth, yet the proper adaptation of the apparatus to the various uses which the public require is often extremely difficult. Indeed, it is only by long experience, and a close application to the business in which I am engaged, that I have become successful; and I am free to confess that I have often made failures in my first attempts at ventilation; but in no instance have I ever abandoned a task which I had undertaken until I succeeded to the satisfaction of myself and employer. There are many important points which must not be overlooked in arranging plans for ventilation; for the adaptation of the means to the end varies with the place and locality—varies also with the character of the ventilation required. There are many details which need

special attention, as, for example, the calibre of the ventilating pipes; the best position of the pipes in relation to the
apartment to be ventilated; the proper adjustment of them
in those cases in which from necessity they require to be
partly horizontal; and the proper arrangement or adjustment also of their orifices, which is a matter of the very
first importance.

It is not common for individuals engaged in a specialty
to speak of failures in their business or profession, but I
prefer to do so. Many years ago the well-known Mr. Ives,
the proprietor of the Albemarle Hotel, in New York City,
employed me to ventilate his larder or provision house for
a stipulated sum. I made several failures in the attempt,
known only to myself, and expended five times as much
money as I was to receive for the work. Finally, however,
I succeeded, to the entire satisfaction of Mr. Ives, and his
card of commendation may be seen among my testimonials
in another place. Since then he has employed me to ventilate other parts of his house. I make these statements
for no other purpose than to show how much care and
judgment are required to accomplish the work of ventilation successfully.

LEADING POINTS OF THE VENTILATOR.—1. It is simple
in its construction, and never gets out of repair. 2. It requires no skill in its use, and no one to be in attendance,
excepting to light the gas in the lantern. 3. It costs but a
trifle for the gas by which it is kept in operation, and is
therefore extremely economical. 4. It can be readily introduced into any house, building, or inclosure which requires to be ventilated. 5. It will remove the foul air
quickly, and as no other method of ventilation, ever yet
discovered, is capable of doing.

PROFESSOR DRAPER'S MODE OF VENTILATION.—Professor Draper, who is highly distinguished as an author and
a man of science, recently published a Text-Book on Physiology, Hygiene, etc., from which we have taken a motto
for our title-page, and from which, also, we purpose to
make brief extracts in relation to foul, damp air and ventilation. We do this chiefly to show that the mode of ventilation he has pointed out for family emergencies, is trouble-

some and incomplete compared with the plan to which we invite public attention.

"It is said," remarks Prof. Draper in his book, "that in many of the houses in New York the servants first light the fires and pump the water out of the cellars ; though this my be an exaggeration, we all know that a damp cellar is the rule, and a dry one the exception. . . . It is, therefore, very important that the cellar of every house, whether private or tenement, should be properly cleansed, dried, and ventilated during the years when the epidemic diseases are raging, if at no other time. . . . In the winter season the furnace will generally produce a sufficient ventilation of the cellar, and prevent the foul air entering the house ; but in the spring and summer, when cholera commences to rage with the greatest violence, the furnace is then extinguished, and there is no ventilation of the cellar. At this time the danger which impends may to a great extent be avoided by placing a small stove in it, in which a fire should be kept burning continually," etc.

Without assuming to discuss this matter, it must be obvious that a fire can not be kept *continually* burning in a stove without considerable expense, and a great deal of care and trouble in watching the fire. Besides, the fire is liable to go out from the negligence of the servant, and thus the absence of ventilation for a time, and more than likely for a whole night, may constitute the critical moment when the cholera, or some other disease, will number us among its unwilling victims. By the use of our Ventilator we have a perpetual motive power, which will cost but a trifle, and which will be a faithful guardian of our health, so far as ventilation is concerned, whether the servants be asleep or awake. Moreover, the Ventilator will not only furnish an abundant supply of pure air, in place of the foul, damp, and noxious air so aptly described by Prof. Draper, but it will afford an agreeable light to one's cellar without any increase of the heat, which is not needed, to say the least, in summer.

ADVANTAGES OF THE VENTILATOR.—It removes foul air, unpleasant odors, and all noxious gases, as heretofore stated, and furnishes a constant supply of pure air in their place, which should be a primary consideration with all who have a regard for their health, comfort, or lives.

It will furnish a bountiful supply of pure air to one's kitchen, so that one's food will be in a more wholesome condition for use, and if one's wife or daughter should go into the kitchen to superintend culinary or other duties, she can return to the parlor without having the disgusting kitchen odor upon her dress or person. Bishop Hughes has said that every young woman, however wealthy or accomplished, should graduate in the kitchen ; and there is no doubt that young ladies, anxious, as they should be, to become accomplished housewives, would be much more inclined to oversee the affairs of the kitchen if, while there, they could have a sweet and wholesome atmosphere to breathe.

The Ventilator will remove the foul air from every part of your domicile, so that the odors and noxious gases from drains, water-closets, kitchens, damp or wet cellars or basements, and other foul places, will be effectually carried away, along with the unwholesome effluvia from your bodies, and the carbonic acid gas thrown out from your lungs and generated by your gas-burners or petroleum lamps or stoves. Thus, you may sleep sweetly all night in a pure air, which will greatly promote the health of your family, and especially that of your children, who are extremely sensitive to the influences of foul air. Rich furniture, gilded picture-frames, and fresco paintings upon walls and ceilings are frequently injured by foul, damp air, but may be effectually preserved by our mode of ventilation. This alone would more than pay for the cost of ventilation. It may be remembered that in 1863 we were visited by a peculiar atmosphere, which, through its dampness, or otherwise, had the effect to mould the paper upon the walls of houses, and cause it to peel off ; to mar the varnish of the furniture, to mould the carpets, and cause them to rot speedily ; to mould even the pictures ; and in some instances the canvas of the pictures was completely rotted, causing the entire loss of a large number of invaluable pictures. Many houses in New-York City and Brooklyn had to be completely refitted in consequence of the injury sustained through the destructive influence of the atmosphere in question ; and all of this loss and evil might have been counteracted by efficient ventilation, which would have prevented the stagnation of the damp or unwholesome air within the apartments.

The Ventilator removes impure air from *horse stables*, the ammoniacle vapors of which tarnish or destroy the varnish upon carriages, and cause horses to sicken and die. In this respect, therefore, ventilation would be a wise economy.

The Ventilator will prevent the rusting of goods made of steel or iron, stored in basements or other damp places. Thousands of dollars might be saved annually to the merchant dealing in goods of this description by efficient ventilation.

INSUFFICIENCY OF FLUES OR CHIMNEYS AS A MEANS OF VEN-
TILATION—ORIGIN OF CHIMNEYS—DIVIDED FLUES.

Chimneys are an old institution—so old, indeed, that we are unable to determine who was the inventor, or in what country they were first employed. We are told of chimneys in Venice before the middle of the fourteenth century; in Padua, before 1368; and of a certain lord of Padua who came to Rome, and finding no chimneys in the inn where he lodged, because at that time fire was kindled in a hole in the middle of the floor, he caused two chimneys, like those that had long been used in Padua, to be constructed by the workpeople he had brought with him. But the claim of the Italians to the invention of chimneys is questioned upon the supposition that they existed in England as early as the twelfth century. However this may be, chimneys began to multiply during the reign of the Tudors, and the subject becoming invested with a sort of artistic interest, it was said that "the chimney shaft became a prominent and beautiful feature in buildings." A little later on, during the reign of Queen Elizabeth, chimneys were regarded as an indispensable "luxury"—that is the historic word—and apologies were made to visitors if they could not be accommodated with rooms provided with chimneys. Ladies, it is said, were frequently sent out to other houses in which they could enjoy, as already quoted, "the luxury of a chimney." We have sadly deteriorated since the reign of "Queen Bess;" for, although three centuries have elapsed, our houses are so constructed that the existence of a room with a chimney is rather the exception than the rule. Hence, the question has been pertinently asked by a distinguished writer—"When will architects and builders be convinced of the fact that fire-places, as well as human beings require constant supplies of fresh air, and that it is their duty to provide every room with air-channels, placed so as to feed the fire without annoying the inmates?"

Although we have a better ventilation with a chimney than without it, yet it is incumbent upon me to point out the comparatively imperfect ventilation which a chimney usually affords. A chimney or flue is described by Dr. Arnott as a pump—"a sucking or drawing air pump,"—which is relied upon as a means of producing an *upward current* of air, and thereby procuring efficient ventilation. But that it notoriously fails is confirmed by our every day experience. We find houses, stables, and public buildings supplied with chimneys, and yet we do not find good ventilation. I have spoken of the offensive condition of the atmosphere in the stable of Mr. Paran Stevens, and yet there was an ample flue at the head of each stall, with a large trap or ventilator in the skylight. If flues could have been of service, Mr. Stevens ought to have had a good atmosphere in his stable. I have spoken also of the *New-York Bank* as having a number of flues opening into the cashier's room, but without any good result in the way of ventilation. I have ventilated so many foul places in which there were flues or chimneys, that I need no other proof of the total inadequacy of this mode of ventilation.

I have spoken of the *upward currents* of air in chimneys, and if we could have those upward currents continually in motion, the problem of ventilation would be solved, and we should be troubled no more with a foul or vitiated atmosphere. But instead of these upward currents, it is a fact that we frequently have *downward currents*, and here is the real difficulty. Chimneys are not always then a luxury, as in the days of Queen Elizabeth. It has been conceded by many distinguished writers, including Dr. Franklin, that the currents in chimneys are irregular, passing *downward* frequently as well as *upward*. It has been stated that chimneys situated in the north wall of a house do not draw so well at those in the south wall, because when cooled by north winds they are apt to "*draw downwards.*" Dr. Franklin has an elaborate explanation of what he terms the *ascending* and *descending* currents in chimneys, which vary according to the period of the day or particular season of the year. I have frequently satisfied myself of the existence of those downward currents in the flues of horse stables, which I have so frequently ventilated for our wealthy citizens, and in which the atmosphere is usually very offensive. A gentleman of distinction, connected with the New York Historical Society, applied to me to ventilate the rooms of the Society, and stated that, according to his experience and observations, currents of air *come down* flues or chimneys oftener than they *go up*.

A heated flue, it may be remarked, is of course more efficient than one not heated, but even this does not always furnish a good ventilation ; and I desire, in this place, to invite attention to the important fact that heat communicated to a flue or chimney from a stove, furnace, range, or other fire, at a distance from the flue, is far less powerful or efficient for ventilating purposes than heat originating directly *within* the flue. This fact lies at the foundation of all my improvements in ventilation, as will be explained more fully hereafter.

Divided flues, or what perhaps may be termed *double flues*, have had some reputation in this country as a means of ventilation. This, we believe, is an English idea engrafted upon our stock of American notions and devices. It presupposes an out draught of heated air from the interior of a building through one tube or flue, with an insetting current of the colder external air through the other tube. In cold weather we have, without doubt, such a result as this ; but when the external air is only a few degrees colder than that within the building, we believe it is not claimed that the action within the tubes is such as to produce any perceptible ventilation. During the greater portion of the summer, therefore, we should be without ventilation, while in winter we may have such a volume of cold air rushing into our apartments as to render the atmosphere chilly or uncomfortable. The Legislative Hall at Albany was ventilated upon this plan in 1862, but I never understood that the experiment was successful.

PROGRESS OF VENTILATION SINCE THE FIRST ISSUE OF THIS WORK IN 1866—
ADDITIONAL EXPLANATIONS OF THE THEORY—ATMOSPHERIC CONDITIONS—
ZYMOTIC DISEASES—FURTHER EXTRACTS FROM LECTURES BY MORRIS
MATTSON, M. D.—MELANGE OF SCIENCE, ART, PHILOSOPHY, HUMOR, ETC.

GENERAL REMARKS.

We here turn over a new leaf — commence, as the
novelist would say, a new chapter ; for ventilation would
seem to have its epochs as well as history. It is now nearly
18 years since the first edition of this book was published,
and within that time we have attended to numerous orders
in reference to ventilation ; have furnished pure air to a
multitude of domiciles; have ventilated School-houses, Court-
houses and Churches ; have removed the odors from kitchens
and water-closets ; have rendered damp and unwholesome
basements as dry and healthful as rooms upon the second
or third floors of well-constructed houses ; have ventilated
horse stables, which has greatly reduced the bills of veterinary surgeons ; have built a number of large refrigerators or
preserving rooms, which are so essential to families; have
added largely to our stock of experience, but without
changing our views in reference to the vast importance of
ventilation in any of its phases ; have found architects more
ready to co-operate with us than heretofore, which, indeed,
is as much to their advantage as ours; made partial contracts
to ventilate some of the State Capitols, and have had interviews with Congressional Committees in reference to the
ventilation of the Capitol at Washington. These committees have twice reported in favor of contracting with us for
the ventilation of the Capitol; but Congress has never found
time to take up and pass the bills recommended; perhaps for
the want of sufficiently energetic outside influence on our
part.

We desire, furthermore, to give additional explanations of our theory of ventilation, which has not been adequately understood by many individuals; to present a brief outline of our labors for the past twenty three years, bringing particularly into view those points which have a special interest for property-owners, as well as those who seek health and comfort in their residences and places of business, through the introduction of pure air; and to fill up our allotted space with "*Arm-Chair Gleanings*" from newspapers, magazines, literary and scientific works, and other sources, in which we have found allusions to the subject of ventilation, or discussions of atmospheric conditions having relation to health and disease. All this will be a pleasant labor for us, and we hope it will prove interesting and profitable to our readers.

FURTHER EXPLANATIONS OF OUR THEORY AND PLAN OF VENTILATION.

In the previous editions of our book, the explanations of our theory of ventilation have not been sufficiently explicit, and we proceed, therefore, to give further information upon the subject. The reader is referred to the figures or illustrations in the first part of our book. Opposite to the title-page is to be seen what is termed "Gouge's Atmospheric Ventilator," consisting of a Ventilating Lantern, an Argand burner, and the necessary air-ducts, both inlet and outlet. This portion of our apparatus may be highly finished, or otherwise, according to the expense which the party using it may be disposed to incur.

The Lantern serves to give light as well as to aid in the process of ventilation, and is very useful for that purpose in cellars, basements, and other dark places, and particularly in powder-magazines, in which this light may be used with entire safety.

INDUCTION OF AIR, ETC.—On the third page is a figure showing how currents of air may be induced, which lies at the foundation of our ventilating process. Without an adequate motive power to establish up-moving currents of air, there can be no efficient ventilation. Our plan is simple, and almost devoid of expense, after the necessary apparatus has been properly adjusted. We do not need a steam-engine to force the air into or out of a building. A simple Argand burner, consuming about a foot of gas to the hour, in connexion with a proper system of inlet and outlet flues or air-ducts, will produce the requisite movements of the air, and secure thorough ventilation in a building of moderate size. A larger building will require a larger amount of gas.

The heating of a flue or chimney with a jet of gas, a kerosene lamp, a stove, or a coil of steam-pipes, as many people have supposed, will not produce ventilation. The peculiar construction and arrangement of the air-ducts, and the adaptation of them to the building to be ventilated, are matters of great nicety. The air-ducts are of variable sizes, and unless the larger and smaller ones have a proper and definite relation to each other, in accordance with the place to be ventilated, the induction of the air will be imperfect, and consequently the ventilation will also be imperfect. This is the reason why certain architects, who have undertaken to ventilate buildings on our plan without consulting us, have made such wretched failures. The force of an induced current of air has a strict relation to the capacities of the flues through which it is made to pass.

When we can do so, we carry our metallic flues in a perpendicular line to the top of the house, above the roof; but if there should be intervening closets, bath-rooms, or water or gas pipes, we are obliged to pass off horizontally until we get free from the obstruction, and this increases the difficulty of rendering the apparatus perfect in its practical workings. Sometimes we are not obliged to ascend to the roof of the house in order to obtain a suitable outlet, and when this is the case, considerable expense is saved to the property-owner in the construction and adaptation of our apparatus.

WEATHER-CAPS.—Figures of these will be found on the fourth page of our book. They are varied in form, so as to be in harmony with the building to which they are attached. They are essential to the proper working of our apparatus, and require care and skill in their construction and adjustment; for, while they prevent the admission of rain, snow, or wind, they must allow of the free exit of the up-moving cur-rents of air from the interior of the building.

COST OF VENTILATION.

This depends, as a matter of course, upon the place to be ventilated, and the amount of ventilation required. The cost, of necessity, is a considerable item, in any case of ven-tilation, as we have to employ the most skillful and expen-sive workmen, and purchase the best quality of tin plate, galvanized iron, and other materials, in the construction of our apparatus. We never use inferior metal, nor allow inferior work to pass from our hands. Nevertheless, we are careful to make moderate rather than extravagant charges, and although, once in a while, an individual may complain of our bill, he would not, after using our apparatus for a week or two, part with it for ten times the cost.

The ventilation of a house of medium size, including the kitchen, parlors, closets, sleeping-rooms, and cellar or base-ment, will vary from $500 to $1,200. The kitchen alone may be about $150; the water-closets alone from $150 to $200. If there is no difficulty in getting an outlet from the building, the expense is always greatly diminished.

The ventilation of a small office will cost from $150 to $250; a banking-house, from $300 to $600.

In school-houses we ventilate five or six of the rooms through one outlet, and the cost of each room varies from $75 to $100.

A church will vary from $1,000 to $2,500.

A preserving-room or provision closet, if built in accord-ance with our directions, we usually ventilate for about $150. The cost will be somewhat increased if there is a diffi-culty in getting an outlet from the building.

HEAT AND VENTILATION.

When employed to ventilate a house or building, we always use the heating apparatus which we find on the premises. We never meddle with the heating arrangements, excepting in some instances to modify the air-ducts through which air is admitted from the exterior of the building.

CO-OPERATION WITH ARCHITECTS.

It is incumbent upon architects to decide all matters pertaining to the ventilation of buildings, and also to decide upon the merits of all new theories or systems of ventilation. It seems appropriate, therefore, that we should address to them these passing remarks. They have an important mission to fulfill. They have even more to do with the health and lives of people, without seeming to be aware of the fact, than physicians themselves. Physicians are only called upon to cure disease, or to patch up the human system as well as they know how; but it should be the province of architects to prevent disease, which will yet be regarded as a higher branch of professional skill. The old but homely maxim, "An ounce of prevention is worth more than a pound of cure," should not be forgotten. To architects are referred the construction of our dwellings, and so long as imperfect ventilation is one of their characteristics, health will be impaired and life shortened. Pure air is the grand panacea by which health is to be maintained. The deprivation of it in our social and industrial relations is one of the greatest evils of our day and generation, and the evil will not be remedied until the construction of our buildings is modified and improved. The public will naturally look to architects for the consummation of this important matter, and the requirement is as just as it is natural. If death should ensue as a consequence of foul air, as it does much more frequently than is imagined, why should not the architect be held accountable for the disaster, just as railroad managers should be held accountable for the lives they destroy through the careless or reckless performance of their duties.

ARCHITECTS SLOW TO CO-OPERATE.—We are free to acknowledge that architects have been tardy in adopting our system of ventilation. We are not surprised at this. Men are not always disposed to examine into new discoveries or inventions. They are apt to cling pertinaciously to preconceived opinions and prejudices. We need not travel far for an example. Take the case of the Abbé Moigno in respect to the *Stereoscope*. He undertook—so goes the story—to introduce the Stereoscope into France. He went to Arago, and other distinguished men of science, for a favorable endorsement. Not succeeding as he desired, he went to the famous

M. Biot. Here again he was disappointed. M. Biot was an enthusiastic defender of a certain theory of light, and would not examine the new instrument through fear that it might contradict the theory in question.

SKEPTICISM OF ARCHITECTS.—We are not surprised, however, that architects should be skeptical with regard to theories or systems of ventilation. They know that millions of money have been expended fruitlessly in this and other countries in experimental ventilation. They have read ponderous volumes upon the subject, abounding in seductive theories and "glittering generalities," but they have derived no benefit from their perusal. They have been unable to reduce the theories to practice. Theoretical ventilation was plausible in the extreme, but practical ventilation proved to be a mystical and unsolved problem. Such has been the experience of the age. Had the numerous volumes on ventilation been of a practical character, buildings would long ago have been supplied with pure air with the same facility that they are now supplied with water, heat and light. But instead of this desirable condition of things, we may look almost in vain for a house or building efficiently ventilated. We may find "ventilating flues," sky-lights, trap-doors in the roof, and other paraphernalia, but we do not ordinarily find pure air. This does not seem to belong to the category of domestic or social comforts. If fresh air gets into a house it is through crevices, or open doors and windows. It surely does not gain admission through the agency of "ventilating flues," or other similar divices. In the midst of such difficulties, with so little to convince the judgment of architects, and still less to stimulate them to practical efforts in the business of ventilation, we do not wonder that many of them should think lightly of our system, or refuse to bestow upon it an investigation.

OUR FIRST EFFORTS.—Notwithstanding what we have just stated, we have made rapid progress in the business of ventilation, albeit our initial success was not achieved through the assistance of the architects. Property owners, and others to whom ventilation was indispensable, sought us out, and were willing to test our new system. Thus, we were encouraged to go forward. Our efforts were of a varied character. We labored for all sorts of people, and in reference to all sorts of business. The pork-packers, among others, applied to us for assistance, as they had heavy interests at stake, and a heavy amount of capital involved in their business. We enabled them to cure their pork more efficiently than heretofore, and without the incidental losses, amounting frequently to thousands of dollars, to which they had been subject. The proprietors of restaurants came to us, through their urgent necessities, and we introduced fresh air into their saloons and refrigerators, which they greatly appreciated. We had opportunities occasionally to ventilate kitchens, parlors, sleeping-rooms, stables, counting-rooms, and banking-houses, which we always succeeded in doing to the satisfaction of our employers. Parties whom we had served would generally take pleasure in recommending us to their friends or neighbors. Through influences of this character our system of ventilation was gradually extended among the people. Occasionally, also, our employers have directed their architects to call upon us in consultation, and in this way some of the leading architects have become the advocates of our system.

SPECIALTY OF THE ARCHITECT—OUR APPARATUS, ETC.— The business of the architect is a *specialty* with which we have never interfered. His supremacy in this particular department of art and science we have always cheerfully acknowledged. At the same time the business of ventilation is equally *our* specialty, and we desire to be without interference also, particularly as we know that it is not likely to prove profitable to the intermeddling parties. Our apparatus is not a whirligig or plaything, and can not be put into use by individuals who have had no experience in its construction and adaptation. It is a combination of parts which can not be made properly or perfectly excepting by trained hands, nor can the parts, after they are made, be adjusted in a building in a proper manner, excepting by those who have had thorough experience in the business. The parts of our apparatus may be enumerated as follows: 1. Ventilating-lantern, with a gas-burner, or other equivalent light. 2. Small metallic air-ducts or tubes, inlet and outlet. 3. Upper and lower registers. 4. Large metallic air-ducts or flues, terminated above the roof by weather caps.

In reference to the parts just enumerated, we have already explained that particular attention must be given to the construction and arrangement of the air-ducts, both large and small, or the induction of the air will be imperfect, and consequently the ventilation will be imperfect, or perhaps altogether deficient. (See page 127) We deem it proper to repeat that the heating of an ordinary flue or chimney with a jet of gas, a stove, or a coil of steam-pipes, will not produce adequate ventilation, although some intelligent people, and even a few of the architects, have been led to suppose that such would be the result. Large sums of money have been foolishly expended in experiments of this description. See the letter of Vincent Tilyou, Esq., page 154

CO-OPERATION BENEFICIAL.—There are a number of architects who now co-operate with us in the construction of buildings which are to be ventilated. They are responsible only for their architectural plans or devices, while we are exclusively responsible for the results of our ventilating arrangements. The co-operation is beneficial in many obvious particulars, and relieves the architects, as they are all free to admit, of a heavy weight of responsibility in respect to the ventilation.

MODE OF CO-OPERATION.—The architect furnishes to us the plan of a building to be erected, with instructions as to the portions of it to be ventilated, and we, in turn, furnish to him a plan of the ventilating arrangements which will be necessary for the purpose. All this may be done efficiently even though the architect and the building may be at a remote distance. Our apparatus will be constructed in accordance with our plans or drawings, and duly forwarded when the building is ready for its reception. It will be accompanied by one of our assistants, who will superintend its adjustment, so that nothing may be wanting to render it accurate and perfect. If a house or building already constructed is to be ventilated, it is only necessary to furnish a plan or drawing of the same, as already directed. We make professional visits, however, to the remotest part of the country, when this is required.

FLUES OR CHIMNEYS.—In the original construction of buildings which are to be ventilated, the architect arranges the necessary flues or chimneys in accordance with his own judgment. We do not now avail ourselves of the smoke flues for the purpose of ventilation. We have found that metallic air-ducts, unconnected with the smoke-flues, are better suited to ventilating purposes. We do not ordinarily find any difficulty in locating the air-ducts after a building has been erected, but they can be arranged to better advantage previously to the construction of the building.

PRESERVING ROOMS.—These have been termed in the first editions of our book *Provision Closets* and *Large Refrigerators*. They vary in size, and sometimes occupy the space of a common sleeping-room. They are even more difficult to ventilate properly than a public or private building. We shall not enter into a description of those difficulties here, nor is it necessary that we should do so. We construct and ventilate *Preserving Rooms* when required to do so by architects, property-owners, or families, and warrant them to be perfect in their operation. We often hear of large sums of money being expended fruitlessly by carpenters, and others, in attempts to construct Preserving Rooms. They are of but little value when they emit a strong odor upon opening the door, or will not preserve meat, and similar articles, more than two or three days in hot weather. There is nothing in the whole range of our business that elicits more enthusiastic praise than our Preserving Rooms.

ORIGIN OF GOUGE'S VENTILATION, INCLUDING OTHER FRAGMENTARY SKETCHES FROM LECTURES BY MORRIS MATTSON, M. D.

The fact that our name is mentioned in these fragmentary sketches, taken from the lectures of Dr. Mattson, from which we have previously quoted (*vide* page 14), is no good reason, perhaps, why we should not give them a place in Part Second of our book, as they relate to topics of vital importance in connection with the subject of ventilation.

NEW DISCOVERIES.—This is a scientific, progressive and practical age; an age, withal, of discovery and invention; and it is somewhat remarkable that the dry details and maxims of science, as they used to be regarded by the common people, have ceased to be the exclusive property of learned professors and cloistered students, but are now comprehended by large masses of the people, many of whom do not claim to be learned, and who are turning their knowledge to good account, thereby enhancing our domestic and social pleasures, and even exercising a potent, though perhaps unconscious, influence upon our civilization.

We not unfrequently observe the most humble and even unlettered individuals making new applications of the truths and principles of science, and deducing therefrom new and important discoveries, which would not have been dreamed of by learned professors or profound philosophers. Hence it is that our every-day experience is teaching us not to be surprised when we are presented with new and valuable discoveries and inventions by those in the middle ranks of life, who have never been the recipients of academic or collegiate honors.

We have made these remarks chiefly in reference to the new, interesting, and important system of ventilation introduced to the public by Mr. Gouge. He is not a member of any learned profession, and yet his discoveries in ventilation were made after such distinguished men as Franklin, Count Rumford, Arnott, Reid, Treadgold, Farraday, and many others had been supposed to exhaust the subject. He has not only announced his discovery in a quiet and unpretending way, but he has reduced it to practice, which is better, as it enables the public to participate in its benefits. Theoretical ventilation is a very different thing from practical ventilation. We are indebted to Mr. Gouge for practical ventilation. His discovery, it would seem to us, is not less important to mankind than the invention of the steamboat, telegraph, or sewing machine. Human progress, in all of its phases, is measured by the health and vigor of the people, and they can have neither health nor vigor without pure air to breathe, and this pure air they can not obtain in their dwellings or places of business, in which they are obliged to pass the most of their time, unless they have adequate ventilation.

The importance of pure air, in relation to health, was one of the earliest dreams of our professional life. In a large medical work, first published in 1841, we devoted a chapter to pure air and ventilation. We were, however, only a neophyte in this important matter. How ventilation was to be accomplished, except by opening the doors and windows, we could not learn from any of the works upon the subject, and we found no adequate solution of the problem until we stumbled upon Mr. Gouge, at his office in Broadway, many years ago.

ORIGIN OF GOUGE'S DISCOVERY—CAVERNS, AND THEIR ANOMALIES.—Having made the acquaintance of Mr. Gouge, we proceeded at once to "interview" him, somewhat after the style of our present energetic newspaper reporters. We said to him, "Mr. Gouge, what first led you to make discoveries in ventilation?" He replied that the subject had always been one of interest to him, but he had never thought of devoting himself to it professionally until one day he was accidentally perusing an account of the wonderful caverns existing in various parts of the world. The lessons which they seemed to teach were deeply impressive, and never to be forgotten. He referred to an interesting work, entitled "Wonders of the Earth and the Heavens." "Many of the caverns therein described," said Mr. Gouge, "vary greatly in their temperature, and exhibit the anomaly of being cold when the external air is warm, or vice versa." A cavern in Hungary, for example, is described as being warm in winter, while in summer the cold is so intense as to produce large icicles, which hang from the roof in grotesque figures; meanwhile, the heat of the sun, outside of the cavern, is almost insupportable. It is also mentioned that the greater the heat without, the more intense is the cold within, so that during the hot weather of dog days, ice is formed copiously within the cavern, which the inhabitants use for cooling their liquors.

Mr. Gouge found in these remarkable contrasts in nature ample material for reflection. The phenomena of evaporation, heat and cold, and atmospheric currents, were all suggestive and instructive. The germ of a new idea was here developed. The brief and incidental study of anomalous caverns, with their strange and inscrutable mysteries, proved to be unconsciously the starting-point of one of the most useful discoveries of the age. By intuition, or some other process of the mental powers, a new theory of ventilation was forced upon the mind of Mr. Gouge. He pondered upon the unbidden revelation (so incomplete, and yet so grand in its conception, coming and going like a shadow,) for days, weeks, months, and years, putting it slowly and cautiously into practice, watching it in all of its complicated details, taking courage under difficulties, profiting by his errors and misconceptions, meeting ridicule and opposition with a determined resistance, and plodding wearily on through every doubt, every misgiving, every obstacle, until his dark and shadowy path became illuminated by the golden sun of success. He has indeed achieved results of the most flattering character, and we need only add how truly it has been said by Bulwer, in one of his novels, that minutes make the hues with which years are sometimes colored.

VENTILATION—EXPERIMENTAL FAILURES, ETC.—There have been numerous books written upon the subject of ventilation, and some of them by able and distinguished authors, recommending various theories and systems of ventilation, and millions of money have been expended during the last quarter of a century in fruitless attempts to obtain a perfect ventilation. Without particularizing, I need only refer to the Capitol at Washington, which is proverbial for its foul and unwholesome air, although, in 1866, it was ventilated under the direction of eminent scientific men, who availed themselves of all the resources of art and science in endeavoring to accomplish their object.

The fact that there have been failures in high places in respect to the systems or processes of ventilation, only shows that we should examine the subject very critically, and assure ourselves, if possible, of the best means of producing a perfect ventilation.

We may congratulate ourselves that the public are beginning to understand that fresh air is indispensable to health. This will ultimately compel architects to construct dwelling-houses upon a different plan. They are now very careful to provide heat, light, water, and bathing facilities, but they do nothing to provide fresh air. They seem to think that all the air we need will come to us through brick walls. Fresh air would seem to be a luxury which even money can not purchase. You may visit the most elegant mansions in our city, and you will often find that they are pervaded by foul odors and noxious gases from the kitchens, laundries, and water-closets. This is due to their faulty construction. You will often find also that a pestilential atmosphere is constantly oozing up into the apartments from the cellar or basements. This is dangerous to health, and should not be tolerated by those who can afford to have their houses ventilated.

CARBONIC ACID GAS.—When the subject of ventilation is discussed, we usually hear much said in relation to carbonic acid gas, as though that were the chief constituent of a foul or unwholesome atmosphere. This is not so, as I shall presently explain. The carbonic acid gas being heavier than common air, it is often supposed that it is precipitated to the floor as fast as it escapes from the lungs, during the process of respiration. It would be unfortunate, indeed, if this were true. Nature has provided against this difficulty through the well-known law which regulates the diffusion of gases. This has been well explained by familiar chemical experiments known to you all. If, for example, you fill a rubber bag with carbonic acid gas, and close it tightly, the whole of the gas will have escaped in twenty-four hours, and the common air will be found in its place. It is stated by Professor Wells, in his work on Chemistry, that if this law of diffusion were suspended, the heavy carbonic acid would accumulate under the influence of gravitation, as a bed or layer in the lower part of the atmosphere, and render the immediate surface of the earth uninhabitable. Carbonic acid gas will permeate a brick wall. The distinguished Pettenkofer is authority for this. He found the gas to escape from an unventilated room by diffusion through its walls. Hence we can not fail to see that the carbonic acid, resulting from combustion and respiration, as well as every other noxious gas or poison, should be speedily discharged from our apartments by an efficient ventilating process.

There are numerous facts going to prove that carbonic acid gas diffuses itself in the atmosphere, and is not precipitated to the floor or surface of the earth, in consequence of its being heavier than the air. De Saussure noted the presence of carbonic acid in the atmosphere of the summit of Mont Blanc, in the region of perpetual snow, and he states explicitly that the proportion of carbonic acid is greater on the tops of mountains than in the plains or valleys. This view has been confirmed by Gay Lussac, who made experiments upon air collected during his aerostatic journey. We quote these authorities from the Congressional report on warning and ventilating the Capitol at Washington, published under the auspices of Prof. Henry, and other scientific gentlemen.

In the above report mention is made of an observer by the name of Loppens, who made experiments upon the air of a theatre at Ghent, and who found that the carbonic acid of an unventilated room is uniformly diffused therein, excepting a slight difference in favor of the ceiling, rather than the floor, "as was ignorantly assumed heretofore from the superior specific weight of this gas." Here is a truth in pungent and decisive words.

While therefore it is admitted, upon high authority, that the carbonic acid is diffused through the atmosphere of a room, with a surplusage of it at the ceiling, instead of being precipitated to the floor, on account of gravity, it must also be admitted that the other foreign and noxious gases, which may be present, are equally diffused in the atmosphere, in obedience to the same unerring law of diffusion. The facts here presented must not be overlooked, as they are intimately connected with Mr. Gouge's system of ventilation. Indeed, we all know that the foulest air of a room, crowded with people, is at the ceiling. Any one who has gone from the lower floor of a crowded theatre, or church, to the galleries, or upper tiers, will bear testimony to this. In the Capitol at Washington, also, the air at the ceiling is represented as being infinitely more foul and disgusting than upon the lower floors, where the members are seated.

It is not to be denied that there is a point of saturation, so to speak, when the carbonic acid will cease to diffuse itself in the atmosphere, and be precipitated to the floor by the force of gravity. We see this in deep wells, where it displaces the atmosphere, and also in close rooms in which charcoal is ignorantly burned for the purpose of warmth. But this precipitation does not take place until the gas has diffused itself in the atmosphere, far beyond that limit which would be safe for individuals to breathe.

In Mr. Gouge's ventilating arrangements, there is in each room an opening in the air-ducts at the floor and ceiling, commanded by registers, which experience has shown to be indispensable to good ventilation. The light and offensive atmosphere, which has been shown to prevail in excess at the ceiling, passes through the upper opening into the ventilating shaft or air-duct, instead of being drawn downward below the zone of respiration. This is practically correct, and will no doubt be found to be philosophically true.

ORGANIC POISON OF THE BREATH.—Critical attention should be given to this branch of our subject. In addition to the carbonic acid gas which escapes from the lungs in the breathing process, there is free nitrogen, abundant aqueous vapor, epithelial scales from the mouth and air-passages of the lungs, and a certain organic matter, existing in some form not yet definitely understood. To this organic matter we invite particular attention. It is conceded to be a poisonous product, and is intensely so in a concentrated form. Added to water, and allowed to remain a certain time, it becomes very offensive. Chemical tests show it to be nitrogenous. It has been collected in sponges by the pains-taking Prof. Bernard, of the College of France, in experiments upon animals. In this concentrated form, it was found to be as deadly in its effects as the noted wourali, or the poison of the viper. Applied to an abraded surface, it produces an intense and dangerous inflammation.

If this organic poison, which diffuses itself in the atmosphere, in connection with the other products of respiration, should be unduly retained in a close apartment, as it always is in the absence of efficient ventilation, it will prove injurious to the health, or give rise to some dangerous or fatal form of disease. It accumulates largely in all crowded places, and is the deadly upas of the School-room, the Church, the Theatre, the Opera, and the Lecture-room. It was this poison that aided in the destruction of so many lives in the fatal Black Hole of Calcutta. We have long believed that it engenders a large amount of disease, without the cause being suspected. The carbonic acid, of which so much is said in discussing the subject of foul air, is the merest bagatelle in comparison with this organic poison.

Cavarret, a French observer, has made some interesting experiments in reference to this poison of the breath. He separated from the atmosphere of a close room, rendered impure by the breathing process, all of the carbonic acid, and other products of respiration, excepting the above organic matter, which he retained. He then exposed certain small animals in the remaining atmosphere, which he found to be slowly poisoned, and ultimately destroyed. Is it not reasonable to suppose, therefore, that thousands of individuals are slowly poisoned in a similar manner, in their sick rooms, without it being suspected that foul air has anything to do with their maladies? The answer must be in the affirmative, or there is no truth in the doctrine put forth by the medical profession in reference to what they call "zymotic diseases." (See page 51.)

This view of the case is confirmed by a lecture delivered before the Royal Institution, in Great Britain, on the relations of town architecture to public health. Dr. Drewitt, the lecturer, stated that close bed-room air was an efficient cause of scrofula and consumption. Thirteen contagious diseases, producible at will, were enumerated. The lecturer expressed his belief that in time epidemic diseases would be made subject to human control, and he thought that the surest mode of protecting the dwellings of the rich would be to cleanse and ventilate the dwellings of the poor.

Cavarret also observed that the carbonic acid of a close, unventilated room, would speedily escape into the external air when the door and windows were opened, but not so with the organic matter, which would remain for many hours, imparting to the atmosphere that peculiar smell which is so characteristic, and so readily detected. It is well enough to remember, therefore, that in entering a close room, in which the air has been rendered impure by respiration, it is not the carbonic acid that we smell, but the organic matter described above, which clings to the atmosphere with great tenacity, and which can not be removed without efficient ventilation.

THE BRAHMIN AND THE MICROSCOPE—THE ATMOSPHERE OF CROWDED ASSEMBLIES.—It is related that Ehrenberg, the great Prussian microscopist, was traveling in India, where he fell into conversation with a Brahmin, whose religious faith forbade him to take life of any kind, or to eat anything which had ever possessed life. Ehrenberg, wishing to demonstrate to the Brahmin the absurdity of his belief, exhibited to him a single drop of water, through the magnifying power of the microscope, in which he saw a countless number of animalculæ. "Alas!" said the poor Brahmin, in despair, "you have destroyed my happiness and my life also; for I see now that I shall never be able to drink, and must perish with thirst."

If the gay and fashionable people who crowd our lecture-rooms, theatres, churches, and other public places, forming a dense mass of human beings, could see the air they breathe, as the Brahmin saw the drop of water, they would, no doubt, shrink instinctively from taking such a polluted atmosphere into their lungs. Two or three thousand people are not unfrequently crowded together in our public places of resort, and, in such a throng, there is always a large number who are more or less diseased. Some will have disease of the lungs; some, inflammation or ulceration of the throat; some, decayed teeth, incrusted with tartar, and alive with animalculæ; some, an ancient catarrh, invading the nasal cavities, and emitting a horrible stench. The blended odors of tobacco and rum will not be wanting. Every breath given out from the lungs of such individuals is heavily laden with foul miasms, or disgusting odors. The exterior as well as the interior of the body will often be found diseased, covered perhaps with fetid ulcers, which would frighten any one but a hospital nurse or surgeon, provided the bandages or dressings could be removed, so as to bring them into view. The unwashed feet and hose of scores or hundreds of very decent-looking and perhaps elegantly-dressed people, to be found in the crowd, also assist in diffusing an odor that would unsettle the stomach of any one not bred in a slaughterhouse, or accustomed to the daily stench of a New York bone-burning establishment. We have noticed this disgusting odor of unwashed feet so frequently in public assemblies, that we are never particularly anxious about any manifestation of applause, which is usually made with the feet; for, although it is pleasant to know that an audience is delighted with an entertainment, the pleasure is more than counterbalanced by the unsavory odor which arises from the floor as a consequence.

In addition to the foul emanations from the bodies of those who are congregated together, we are not to overlook the carbonic acid gas which is exhaled from the lungs. We have stated elsewhere that from twelve to fifteen hundred cubic inches of this gas is discharged from the lungs of a healthy adult every hour. Let us say twelve hundred cubic inches, so as to have a tolerably fair average, and multiply this by one thousand, which will represent a moderate New York audience, and we shall have one hundred and twenty thousand cubic inches of the gas exhaled in a single hour. With this excessive quantity of the gas, which can not make its escape for the want of ventilation, is blended the fetid and disgusting odors already mentioned, until we have an atmosphere totally unfit to be breathed by any human being, or indeed by any of the lower animals, and which no person of intelligence or discretion would breathe, if he had a just conception of its true nature and character, any more than the Brahmin would drink water, in opposition to his religious faith or convictions, after he had found it to be teeming with animal life.

DRINKING FROM THE SAME CUP.—People are so dainty that no two of them will drink from the same cup without having it previously washed, as though they feared that some infectious matter might be imparted by the lips; and yet they have no hesitation in breathing air which a multitude of persons have been filtering through their lungs, until it has become polluted and unfit for the purposes of respiration. Go to the New York Central Park, of a summer afternoon, where the high and the low, the rich and the poor, are assembled in crowds, and observe how carefully each thirsty pedestrian, in drinking at one of the fountains, will rinse the cup before touching it to his lips, as though apprehensive of being poisoned. Observe, again, a little later in the day, how those dainty people rush into the avenue cars, on their return home, crowded together in a dense mass, and breathing without apparent fear or concern, a pestiferous atmosphere, in which there is enough of filth and poison to sicken a whole regiment of Libby or Andersonville troops.

A further illustration of this curious anomaly may be observed at table during meals. Woe to the landlord or landlady if a speck of dirt is seen in contact with any of the food placed before the guests. Disgust or indignation would be instantly manifested, as if an unpardonable sin had been perpetrated. And yet if those delicate people were gifted with microscopic eyes, so as to observe equally well the impurities of the air they are frequently compelled to breathe, how much greater would be their disgust and intolerance. Instead of criticising so closely the food which is to enter the *stomach*, they should give a little more attention to the food which is to enter the *lungs*, namely, the pure air of heaven, untainted by odors or miasms, and without a due supply of which life would become almost instantly extinct.

FAINTING IN PUBLIC PLACES.—People have been so long accustomed to foul air that they think very lightly of the matter, or rather, perhaps, they do not think of it at all, for the reason that they have no adequate conception of the unwholesome character of the atmosphere which they are frequently compelled to take into the lungs, especially in public places. Nevertheless, many individuals suffer severely in their visits to public assemblies, being sometimes obliged to leave before the entertainment has closed, in consequence of faintness, headache, or a feeling of stupefaction; or forced to leave, it may be, which indeed not unfrequently happens, because a wife or a daughter has suddenly swooned, and has to be carried into the fresh air. Incidents of this kind ought to teach the public a useful lesson, and yet they seem to be regarded as the merest trifles, and are soon forgotten. We have known many cases of severe and protracted disease, which resulted from breathing the poisonous air of crowded assemblies. There are scores of ladies and gentlemen in every community (and this is true more particularly of those a little advanced in life,) who never visit a crowded assembly, because they know they can not do so without suffering with a headache, or some other ailment. What a comment is this upon the architectural deficiencies of our public buildings.

ARCHITECTS TO BLAME.—It is a great calamity, so far as health is concerned, that there should be a public building, in which crowds of people assemble, without adequate ventilation, whereby each individual present would receive as full a supply of fresh air as though he were the inhabitant of some mountain range. It is a marvel, indeed, with all of the progress which we have made in the arts and sciences, with all of the knowledge which we have of the truths of physiology and hygiene, that we should be so sadly deficient in the art and science of ventilation, which is infinitely more worthy of our attention than architectural adornments, or the costly and beautiful trappings pertaining to a fashionable residence. If it be criminal to destroy life with a murderous weapon, why may it not be considered equally criminal to destroy life by means of the foul air which is allowed to accumulate in public or private buildings in conseqence of inadequate ventilation ?

INFERIOR PHYSICAL DEVELOPMENT, ETC.—*Foul air*, which is synonymous with *deficient ventilation*, exercises a blighting influence upon both the vegetable and animal kingdoms. Plant a potato in a dark cellar, and it will send up a long white stem, entirely devoid of any green color. It is only the pure air and the sun-light that can impart to it the usual characteristics of growth and color. So with the human body. Take from it the pure air, and it will suffer in growth and development. This is no hypothesis. According to medical testimony, submitted to the House of Commons in 1840, the children of the English silk-weavers, who pass their lives in a close and confined air, are extremely subject to scrofula and softening of the bones. So says Mr. Tomlinson, in his work on Ventilation. Scrofulous diseases, according to this authority, is a common result of bad ventilation. Children, moreover, born of parents living continuously in bad air, show signs of physical inferiority. Dr. Arnott, the eminent English physician, is quoted as saying, "Defective ventilation deadens both the mental and bodily energies ; it leaves its mark upon the person, so that we can distinguish the inhabitants of a town from those of the country."

Nothing is more true than the statements of Dr. Arnott, and with such facts before us, the inference is conclusive, that the deprivation of pure air, beginning with the nursery, and passing onward through the different stages of life, must tend ultimately to enfeeble even our *national life*. If the stones of a building are not firm and enduring, the building itself will be deficient in those qualities. There is no such a thing as a vigorous nationality, without a vigorous people for its foundation. If we have scrofulous and rickety children, we shall have an infirm and rickety manhood and womanhood, and thus we shall gradually pass into decay, and lose all of our moral, spiritual, and political prestige. Pure air, then, is not only the foundation of good health, but it is the foundation of virtue, of morality, of religion, of heroism, of a pure and elevated manhood, of all that can beautify, advance, or strengthen our civilization.

BISMARCK — SHIP-VENTILATION. — It would seem that this distinguished statesman is not satisfied with having been instrumental in merely ventilating some of the European governments, if we may speak figuratively, but is equally desirous of employing a similar remedy in case of the ill-starred emigrant ships which occasionally set sail from the Prussian dominions. At all events, a noble pledge was given by Bismarck, during the past year, while acting as Prime Minister, to co-operate with the Prussian Government in preventing the repetition of such cases as that of the emigrant-ship Liebnitz, in which there was such a melancholy loss of life by the cholera.

But how the repetition was to be prevented, or what was to be the remedy of the great statesman, we have never been informed. If he believes in *atmospheric ventilation*, as he evidently believes in *governmental ventilation*, and should make a proper application of the remedy, we should hear no more of deaths from foul air on ship-board, nor of the ravages of ship-cholera and ship-fever, a consummation devoutly to be wished.

Bismarck is a progressive man, but whether he has made sufficient progress to enable him to discover that *fresh air* is as indispensable to a healthy physical life, as *good government* is indispensable to a healthy national life, is more than we can tell. It is amazing, to say the least, that any enlightened government should permit an emigrant ship to leave its waters without adequate arrangements for a healthful supply of fresh air. The learned men of Prussia, of Europe, and of all Christendom, know that foul air is incompatible with health, and that it is the very pabulum upon which the cholera feeds. Why, then, this indifference to the subject? No individual, no government, has yet taken the initiative in *ship-ventilation*. It is yet among the undeveloped things of the nineteenth century. In this respect, Liebig has written his chemistries in vain. The Colleges and Universities of the civilized world have been teaching chemistry and science to no purpose. The preservation of human life does not seem to be a subject worthy of notice. The poor emigrants crowd into the vessels which are to receive them, full of high hopes, without dreaming that they are in danger of being poisoned to death by foul air, or having their lives cut suddenly short by the cholera or ship-fever. It is fitting, therefore, that Bismarck should do something to prevent this terrible sacrifice of human life. The remedy is simple; the cost would be but a trifle; and yet the phenomenon of a *ventilated ship* crossing the ocean has never yet been witnessed; and if we are to judge from the tardy progress of the age in respect to ventilation, it may not be witnessed for a century to come. If ships visiting our shores from Europe had been properly ventilated, we never should have heard of the Asiatic cholera on this side of the Atlantic. Bismarck, therefore, could not render the United States, nor indeed the whole civilized world, a greater service than by using his potent influence and prestige in having all emigrant ships efficiently ventilated.

HEADACHE—STEINWAY HALL.—Headache is one of the accompaniments of fashionable places of amusement. We have no desire to be invidious in referring to Steinway Hall. It does not differ essentially, in regard to ventilation, from other places of amusement in our city. We refer to it especially, because it is one of the grand centres of gay and fashionable life in our metropolis. Ladies and gentlemen flock there in crowds to attend lectures, readings, concerts, and all sorts of attractive and agreeable entertainments. Clergymen and lawyers—saints and sinners—musical people, and those who are not musical—beautiful women, and some who are not beautiful—all assemble in this noted place. Dickens gave his readings there; Fanny Kemble read her round of Shaksperian characters there; Anna Dickinson, Olive Logan, and Kate Field have lectured there; Carlotta Patti and Parepa Rosa have sung there; the American Institute gave a course of lectures there; Mr. Milburn, the blind preacher, with Gov. Hoffman in the chair, gave one of his eloquent discourses there; in short, everything of a high order in literature, music, art, or science, intended for the New York public, is more than likely to be presented in Steinway Hall. We are justified, therefore, in criticising the place in reference to non-ventilation. The impurity of the air in the Hall is unquestioned. It is apparent at all times, with or without an audience. An individual entering the Hall in the evening, just as the doors are opened, can not fail to detect the peculiar smell of a pent-up atmosphere, which has been poisoned by the human breath. It is this atmosphere which produces the headache, and we are sorry to affirm that there are scores of ladies and gentlemen who can not attend a public entertainment in Steinway Hall without suffering with headache, or some analagous disease. A gentleman is now at our elbow who says he went there with three ladies to hear Carlotta Patti sing. Each of the party, himself included, suffered severely with headache. One of the ladies was from a distant part of the country, and said that she would be unwilling to remain and endure such suffering, but from her desire to hear the singing of Carlotta, which she compared to the warbling of a bird. Such a foul and horrid atmosphere as this should not be permitted to exist in any fashionable place of resort, nor indeed in any other place in which human beings are crowded together.

Mr. Steinway would make many a heart glad by having his Hall properly ventilated. We have not the pleasure of his acquaintance, but we learn that he is liberal in his views, and fully appreciates the necessity and importance of pure air. We are told that he originally had openings made in the ceiling of the Hall for the escape of the foul air, but, unfortunately, the foul air showed no disposition to make its escape. Like a well-fed prisoner, it did not choose to leave its place of confinement. Mr. Steinway then availed himself of what are called "*prism lights*," which he imported from France at a heavy expense, showing a disposition to do all in his power to render the Hall perfect in respect to ventilation. These lights were placed in the ceiling, where they are now to be seen. It was assumed, by those who advised Mr. Steinway in the matter, that the prism lights would be instrumental in ventilating the Hall, but their failure to do so is well known to all who visit the place. The cost of importing the lights could not have been less than $5,000, and we have no hesitation in saying, that if one-fourth of that sum had been paid to Mr. Gouge for the adjustment of his ventilating apparatus, the visitors of Steinway Hall would not now have occasion to complain of the foulness of the atmosphere, or go home from an entertainment suffering with intense headache.

"FORCED VENTILATION"—FANS AND ENGINES.

This is a peculiar kind of ventilation, with a motive power entirely different from that employed by myself, and on that account, as well as from its novelty, I bring it to the notice of the reader. Ventilation, strictly defined, is nothing more nor less than the removal of foul air from a building or other enclosure, and the introduction in its place of pure or fresh air. How simple the proposition! And yet there seems to have been nothing in art or science more difficult to accomplish. It has puzzled the wisest heads, and baffled the skill of our most eminent men. Among the methods devised for realizing this golden dream is that of "forced ventilation," which has its advocates in Europe as well as the United States. We find this new phrase in a document issued by order of the 39th Congress, in relation to the warming and ventilation of the Capitol at Washington. Previous to this, the Capitol had been systematically ventilated, or rather, it had been subjected to the forcing process already mentioned; and the plan adopted for the purpose, according to the document from which we quote, consisted in drawing a given quantity of external air into chambers for its reception by means of fans, when it was warmed by passing among stacks of pipes heated by steam-boilers, and forced into the halls of Congress through apertures in the floors and walls. This has been truly called "*a forced ventilation.*" The column of air thus introduced displaces an equal quantity of vitiated air, which escapes through apertures in the ceiling and the numerous doors leading into the halls and galleries. There are four fans employed for this purpose, operated by steam-engines. The fan for the Senate chamber is described as being 14 feet in diameter, and weighing over *six thousand pounds.* It is moved by an engine of 16-horse power. The fan in the hall of Representatives is 16 feet in diameter, and weighs *nine thousand pounds.* It is moved by a steam-engine of 30-horse power.

One would suppose that those ponderous fans and formidable steam-engines would furnish an abundance of fresh air, and yet it is proverbial that ventilation is sadly deficient in the two houses of Congress. When the Senate-chamber or house of Representatives is crowded, the atmosphere is known to be almost stifling, and certain it is that we have been officially consulted by several congressional committees in reference to the further ventilation of the Capitol.

If we should be employed to render this service, we shall forego the expense of fans and steam-engines, and use only our simple apparatus, which we have found so efficient in ventilating many large public buildings. We will guarantee pure air to the members of Congress, and that too at a merely nominal cost, after the necessary expense has been incurred for the construction and adaptation of our apparatus. We shall take pride, to say the least, in showing to the scientific world, that foul air may be removed from a building, and fresh air made to take its place, without employing such formidable and expensive apparatus as they now have in the Capitol at Washington.

Comparisons, says the noted Dogberry, are odorous. And yet it is sometimes necessary to make comparisons. In doing this, we bring into juxtaposition a huge steam-engine, in connection with a monstrous fan, employed as a motive power in the process of ventilation, and the simple apparatus which we term an "Atmospheric Ventilator," employed for the same purpose, with its silent but steady up-moving currents of air, which operate by night as well as by day, without requiring an engineer or superintendent. It does its work without any wear or tear of machinery, hissing of steam, or other clatter or noise. It does not require the building of anthracite, or other fires. There is no explosion of steam-boilers, or payment of bills for broken wheels, shafts, or other expensive apparatus.

HOME INSURANCE COMPANY—MULTIFORM VENTILATION—

Our book has now reached the 4th Edition, which is greatly enlarged, and which is designed to put the people more than ever upon their guard against the baneful influences of poisoned air. We should consider our book incomplete, however, without a report in reference to the ventilation of the *Home Insurance Company's* office. What we have to say may be regarded as a "twice-told tale," but it is nevertheless full of interest and instruction, so far as fresh air and ventilation are concerned. The office of the Company is at 135 Broadway, New York City. It is devoted to fire insurance, and is the largest institution of the kind, with one exception, in the United States. The president is Charles J. Martin, Esq. It has been in operation over 28 years, and has a capital of $2,000,000. It is located in a spacious building, having a front on Broadway of forty feet, and on Cedar Street of 153 feet. Is is open on all sides, with large and numerous windows, which would lead one to suppose that the air within the building would be tolerably pure, but such has not proved to be the fact. The business of the Company is transacted on the first or main floor, where about forty employees may be observed industriously at work. The rear basement underneath this floor is used as a kitchen and dining-room, where dinner is served to the

employees, and also, when occasion requires, to the directors and officers. The Company took possession of the
building in 1863, and from that time until nearly 1870,
when we established our ventilation, the employees and
officers had suffered severely from the poisoned air. Everything pertaining to the business of the establishment during
that long period—the making out of policies, the declaring
of dividends, and last, though not least, the eating of dinners—has been transacted in an atmosphere surcharged with
noxious gases and other dangerous poisons. Every breath
taken has served to convey something more than an infinites-
imal dose of those poisons into the lungs, and through the
lungs into the blood, to be distributed by the circulation to
every part of the system It is only a wonder that any of the
employees or officers are alive at this moment. Mr. Martin,
the president, who is very sensitive to the influence of foul air,
sought relief in various ventilating experiments which were
recommended to him by interested parties, but in the results
of which he has been more or less disappointed. These
multiform experiments we will notice very briefly in the
order of their adoption.

· *Experiment No.* 1.—This consisted of "ventilating flues,"
such as we have frequently mentioned in this work. There
were at least a baker's dozen of them. They opened in the
ceiling of the main room, and were extended to the roof.
We need scarcely say that they were useless

Experiment No. 2.—In this experiment an additional
flue of a large size was employed, being about thirty inches
square. It was placed in the centre of the room, and opened
like the others in the ceiling. It rendered no service in the
process of ventilation.

Experiment No. 3.—Most unfortunately for the theories
of the architects, neither the *big flue* nor the *little flues*
assisted the ventilation. Under these circumstances it was
decided to rarify the air in the big flue with jets of burning
gas, but this also proved to be a failure.

Experiment No. 4.—Abandoning all hope of ventilation
by flues, an experiment of a different kind was put into
requisition. A stack of steam-pipes, enclosed in a box, was
arranged beneath the sill of a window in the main room.
The box had an aperture at the bottom on the inside, and

another at the top on the opposite side, communicating with the outer air. The steam-pipes being heated, the foul air was expected to flow in at the lower aperture, and make its exit through the upper one into the open air. The device being completed, lighted matches were applied to the lower aperture, but it was found that the currents of air were very irregular; sometimes they moved upward, sometimes downward, and sometimes there were no currents at all. This was the end of Experiment No. 4.

Experiment No. 5.—It was next decided to enter upon a grand experiment upon a somewhat larger scale, which seemed to have unquestionable recommendations, and unquestionable scientific endorsements. In this case the currents of air were to pass *downward* instead of *upward*, constituting what is termed "ventilation from the floor," or "downward ventilation.' In carrying out the project, a large horizontal air-duct, say 14 x 20 inches, made of wood, was placed immediately beneath the floor of the main room. Diverging from this were smaller horizontal ducts connected with registers in the floor. The large duct, pursuing a zigzag course, ultimately terminated in an air-chamber in the basement, heated by a stove. From the air-chamber a large air-duct ascended to the roof, through which the impure air was to be discharged. The stove being heated—we will not stop to calculate the expense of the fuel, nor the wages of a fireman to watch the stove and keep it in working order—it was supposed that the foul air of the apartment above would flow through the registers in the floor into the diverging air-ducts, and proceed onward through the large air-duct into the air-chamber. From this chamber—if there was any faith to be put in theoretical surmises or speculations—the air would inevitably ascend through the connecting air-duct and make its escape into the atmosphere. While the foul air was to be disposed of in this quiet way—flowing downward through the air-ducts as water would flow through a syphon—the fresh air was to descend in abundant streams from the roof through the "ventilating flues" already described. However plausible the theory, the ventilation does not seem to have been satisfactory.

The President, in utter hopelessness, and suffering more or less from poisoned air, applied to me for relief, precisely as a drowning man, according to the old adage, will sometimes catch at straws. He told an amusing story of his experience in ventilation. According to his showing, the foul air which "encompassed him about," was something like a mill-stone, and could not be made to go either up or down. It would not go up through the small "ventilating flues," as the architects all seemed to think it ought to do ; nor through the larger flue in the centre of the main room, even though heated with gas-jets ; nor through the box of steam-pipes under the window-sill, which was a shorter route ; nor downward through the registers in the floor on its way to the stove in the basement. He had lost all faith in the theories of ventilation, as well he might, and was unwilling, as the representative of his Company, to pay out any more money for experiments in ventilation unless success should be guaranteed. Not objecting to his skepticism, we agreed to ventilate the large room on the first floor of the building in question, measuring 40 by 153 feet, as already stated, in a satisfactory manner, for a sum not exceeding two thousand dollars, or forego compensation. Our proposition being accepted, we proceeded to adjust our ventilating apparatus, which was put in operation December 10th. In reference to the results, Mr. Martin, in a letter dated December 31st, 1869, observes, "It affords me pleasure to say that we find a marked and decided improvement in the atmosphere of our office, which is noticed not only by the officers and clerks, but also by the directors and others calling in occasionally ; and we are congratulating ourselves that we have at length found a remedy for the evil which has so long annoyed us."* The clerks referred to by Mr. Martin seem to be very decided in their expressions of approbation. They do not now suffer with headache, languor and depression as they did, and can perform a larger amount of labor without fatigue or exhaustion. In entering the main room from the street, the visitor recognizes a peculiar and agreeable freshness in the atmosphere, which makes an exhilerating impression on the senses, instead of that offensive odor characteristic of a foul and poisoned atmosphere, and which Mr. Chadwick, of England, has truthfully termed the "*dead man's smell.*"

Banking-houses are usually much in need of ventilation, because the directors, cashiers, clerks, and others employed, undergoing much severe labor, need a full and constant supply of fresh air; it is equally important that the poisonous carbonic acid gas which is given off at every breath from their lungs, and the poisonous effluvia also which are exhaled from their bodies, should be carried speedily away from the apartments; for if breathed over and over again, as is always the case where ventilation is deficient, the blood, according to the testimony of physicians, undergoes deterioration, and disease is often an inevitable consequence.

The well-known *New York Bank* may be mentioned as an instance of this imperfect ventilation, which came to my knowledge through the instrumentality of Judge Henry Hilton of New York City, whose stable I had ventilated very much to his satisfaction. Owing to this circumstance he was kind enough to give me a letter of introduction to the cashier of the above bank, the well-known Mr. Meeker, suggesting that it would be well to employ me to ventilate the place. I found that the frequent complaints of its imperfect ventilation were well founded. The atmosphere was extremely close and vitiated. Much had been done to ventilate the place, but all efforts had proved unsuccessful. A number of flues had been constructed so as to open into the cashier's room, with the hope of obtaining adequate ventilation, but it answered no good purpose. I proceeded at once to put my system of ventilation into operation, and it was no sooner accomplished than every person employed in the cashier's room perceived an immediate and almost magical change in the atmosphere. Compared with the depressing influence of the foul air which they had been so long accustomed to breathe, it was like some delicious and renovating ether; and it had the effect, as I am informed, of restoring one of the clerks, who had been for a long time an invalid, to very good health.

A CHAIN WITH MANY LINKS.

This figurative expression is typical of a series of ventilations which have been perfected in New York City, the one growing out of the other, and the whole forming an aggregate which the writer has thought proper to compare to "a chain with many links." There can be no better evi-

dence of the value of a new invention than the rapid
adoption of it by individuals in consequence of hearing it
eulogized by others having it in use. It is in this way that
our "New System of Ventilation" has advanced so rapidly
in public estimation. Those, however, who may still be
skeptical with regard to its merits, as property-owners,
architects, and the heads of families, are referred to the evidence given below in reference to many practical and interesting points connected with the system in question.
Among other things, it will be seen that the value of property may sometimes be greatly enhanced by adopting our
mode of ventilation.

RESTAURANT VENTILATED—PROPERTY QUADRUPLED IN
VALUE.—At the corner of Exchange Place and Hanover
Street is a first-class restaurant, kept by Mr. Hampe. Here
gentlemen congregate to get their lunches and other meals.
The place, however, had many objections, some of which
are common to most of restaurants. Bad odors from
the kitchen pervaded the building, rendering the dining-
room more or less uncomfortable, and causing such a disagreeable stench in the rooms and offices above the kitchen
as to drive the occupants away. Some of the rooms had
been long vacated in consequence of their unpleasant condition. The kitchen, in addition to the "bad smells," was
oppressively hot, so that it was difficult for the cooks to
attend to their duties. In this serious dilemma, Mr. Hampe
applied to me for assistance. I proceeded at once to ventilate the place, and, as soon as my labors were completed,
an almost magical change was observed in the atmosphere.
The heat of the kitchen was reduced to an agreeable temperature, the bad odors were no longer perceptible, the cooks
put on smiling faces, and the dining-room and offices above
the kitchen were rendered sweet and comfortable. Mr.
Hampe was greatly pleased with the result, and seemed
eager to pay my bill as soon as the work was completed.
The rooms and offices which had long been vacated, were
soon filled with occupants. One office alone, in consequence of its improved condition, rented for $1500 per year.

My bill for ventilating Mr. Hampe's place did not exceed
$500, and yet the annual value of the building, in which
it was located, was increased to more than four times that.

ANOTHER RESTAURANT—MORE ABOUT FLIES—SWARMS OF FLIES. —This too was a first-class restaurant, kept by the well-known Mr. Schultz, at 25 William Street. He had heard of the ventilation of Mr. Hampe's establishment, and hence his application to me. I found his place in a deplorable condition. The temperature of his kitchen was 130 degrees, and of course the atmosphere was stifling and oppressive. The cooks and other employees suffered intensely from the heat. Added to the other discomforts, there was a swarm of flies always present. The hot and stifling atmosphere of the kitchen invaded the dining-room, which was upon the same level, and caused many gentlemen, who came for their dinners or lunches, to desert the place. The offices above the dining-room also became impregnated with the hot and foul air from the kitchen, and some of the occupants made strenuous efforts to have Mr. Schultz ejected.

Previous to the conversation with me, an attempt had been made by a certain party to ventilate the place, but without success. Two large flues, made of wood, had been put up and extended to the top of the building, connecting one with the kitchen, and the other with the dining-room. These flues, like all other similar flues, did not answer the purpose. According to Mr. Schultz, the heat in the kitchen continued much the same, the swarms of flies were not abated, and the atmosphere in the dining-room was not improved. He paid the experimenter for his labors, but said that the money had been thrown away.

It was a month or two after this that the application was made to me. Mr. Schultz wished to know whether I could ventilate his place successfully, to which I replied in the affirmative, but he said, "Several have promised the same thing, and I have paid my money without receiving any benefit." He added, in a peculiar foreign idiom—"It's no good.' I said, in reply—"What I do for you shall be successful or I will make no charge. My motto is—No success, no pay." Mr. Schultz was then willing to employ me, and I proceeded at once with the work. The dining-room was first ventilated, and this proving a success, I next proceeded with the kitchen ; next the pastry-room ; and finally, I rearranged and improved an old refrigerator, which I found in a bad condition. Mr. Schultz acknowledged my work to be a success, and gave me his name as a reference. A good atmosphere now pervaded the dining-room ; the heat of the kitchen had been reduced to an agreeable temperature, without the presence of unwholesome odors ; the pastry-room had become acceptable to the operatives, instead of being repulsive ; and meat, with similar articles, could be kept as long as desirable in the refrigerator. The offices above the dining-room ceased to be contaminated with the foul air from the kitchen, so that the occupants no longer made complaints, and did not ask for the expulsion of Mr. Schultz. The swarms of flies also, which had infested the kitchen and dining-room, immediately disappeared upon ventilation being established, showing that there is no at-traction for them in a pure atmosphere.

BANKING-HOUSE — FLUES A NULLITY — SICKNESS FROM FOUL AIR.—The Banking House here spoken of is at 18 Exchange Place. The firm is Dennistown & Co. The man-aging partner is D. P. Sellar, Esq. Mr. Sellar had been in the habit of lunching at the restaurant of Mr. Schultz, and ascertained that the pleasant atmosphere of the dining-room was due to an improved process of ventilation. Obtaining my name and address from Mr. Schultz, he immediately sent for me in consultation. He expressed his satisfaction with the ventilation in the above restaurant, which he said he had examined closely, and wished to know if the princi-ple could be applied to his banking-house. He spoke very emphatically of the foul and unwholesome air of his office, and said that he was obliged to walk half of his time in the street, to the neglect of his business, to avoid getting sick, and, notwithstanding this precaution, he generally went home with a headache. He sought advice with regard to the best means of getting rid of the noxious air which was so detrimental to him, and was told that he would have to employ ventilating flues. There were two flues already in the walls of the building, and, in addition to these, he had two open grates, instead of one, for burning coal, each with its appropriate flue, so that there were four flues altogether, and two of these were heated specially during cold weather by grate fires. Nevertheless, there was no adequate ventilation, and Mr. Sellar was literally driven into the street, according to his own statement, to save himself from sickness.

Mr. Sellar instructed me to ventilate his banking-house without delay, which was done, and as soon as the ventilation was established, he recognized an improvement in the atmosphere. Within a week after this time, he told me he had ceased to be troubled with the headache, and added, "Instead of walking the street much of the time, I now remain in my office all day, attending to my business, and go home in the evening feeling as fresh as when I came in the morning."

DWELLING-HOUSE OF D. P. SELLAR, ESQ.—Through the instrumentality of this gentleman, the links of our metaphorical chain rapidly increased. Enjoying the benefits of pure air in his office during business hours, he recognized the necessity for it in his residence, after business had ceased. He employed me, therefore, to ventilate his kitchen and dining-room, which were to him a source of annoyance. This was done to his entire satisfaction. After a time he went to Europe, and upon his return he employed me to ventilate his parlor, sleeping-rooms, butler's pantry, and halls. These were also done to his satisfaction, so that now he has pure air to breathe in his banking-house during business hours, and at his residence during the hours of relaxation and sleep. The improvement in his health, we venture to predict, will more than compensate for all of the expense he has incurred, and we doubt whether all of the banking-houses in the country could purchase from him the privilege he now enjoys of breathing a healthful atmosphere, whether asleep or awake.

LIVERPOOL, LONDON AND GLOBE INSURANCE COMPANY. —This establishment is in William Street, and is one of the largest and most influential fire insurance companies in the country. We were introduced to the Company by Mr. Sellar, named above. We found a close and foul atmosphere in the rooms, causing the inmates great discomfort. We found also an open grate for burning coal, and "ventilating flues" in the walls. We did not, however, find any fresh air. We speedily adjusted our ventilating apparatus, which gave entire satisfaction to the Company.

UNION CLUB ROOMS — USELESSNESS OF FLUES. — The well-known Union Club occupies a magnificent building at the corner of Fifth Avenue and Twenty-First Street. Among numerous other rooms in the commodious building is a large double parlor, devoted to conversation, cigar-smoking, etc., which was complained of as being extremely uncomfortable. I had a conference in relation to the matter with the President of the Association, Griswold Grey, Esq., to whom I was introduced by Mr. Sellar, so frequently mentioned in these pages, and who is also a member of the Club. I was requested to call in the evening, so as to make myself fully acquainted with the exact condition of the rooms. I found the atmosphere oppressive and stifling, being saturated with cigar-smoke, and rendered still more noxious by the carbonic acid from the brilliant gas-jets by which the parlor is illuminated. The kitchen, also, though remote from the parlor, sent its unwelcome odors thither, and added still further to the discomforts of the atmosphere. I was informed that by eleven o'clock in the evening the air would become so foul and pungent as to cause a copious flow of water from the eyes. It was further stated that the windows could not be opened on account of the draught, and that the insetting currents of cooler air only served to drive the foul air into every part of the building.

Attempts had been made to remedy this unpleasant condition of things, but without success. The well-known "flue ventilation" had been put in requisition, and no less than six of those flues were observable in the walls. The flues, however, as in all similar cases, would not operate as desired, and the beautiful parlor, of which we have spoken, was rendered wholly unfit for the accommodation of gentlemen desirous of enjoying the comforts or pleasures of social life. After a full examination of the place, Mr. Grey said to me, " Can you ventilate these rooms?" Upon my responding in the affirmative, he added, " Are you willing to guarantee success, or, in case of failure, to make no charge for your services?" To this also I responded in the affirmative, as I do in all similar cases, and without further remarks

154

Mr. Grey directed me to proceed with the work. This was speedily executed, and within a fortnight afterwards my bill was covered by a check, which indicated that the work had given satifaction. Since that time I have occasionally seen Mr. Grey, and other members of the Association, and they all agree that the ventilation is in every respect satisfactory.

ARCTIC INSURANCE COMPANY—FLUES AND STEAM-PIPES FAIL TO VENTILATE, ETC.—This Company is at 104 Broadway. Vincent Tilyou, Esq., is the President. I received an introuction to the Company through the Liverpool, London and Globe Insurance Company. This link in our somewhat extended chain is one of great interest and practical importance. The office and rooms of the Arctic Company are a little below the pavement. The President complained seriously of the foul air of the place, and said that it had impaired his health. Various devices had been tried to ventilate the rooms, but, as usual, every experiment had failed. Five or six "ventilating flues" had been tried in vain, and I heard the old and oft-repeated story that the flues would not draw. Sky-lights were superadded, but they gave no relief. Then followed the experiment, which is by no means a new one in the art of ventilation, of putting steam-pipes into the flues. The object of this device was to rarify the air, and produce ascensional currents. But there was no removal of the foul air. It still remained to annoy Mr. Tilyou, as well as the officers and clerks. Continuing to suffer from the confined air, beyond the limit of ordinary endurance, Mr. Tilyou ultimately applied to me for relief. I was to officiate as a doctor in the cure of his maladies; but instead of using medicine for the purpose, I was to employ what was infinitely preferable in his case, the panacea of fresh air.

The following letter of President Tilyou, relating to the ventilation of the Arctic Insurance Rooms, was kindly furnished at our request, and will be read with pleasure by all who are interested in the subject of ventilation.

OFFICE OF THE ARTIC FIRE INSURANCE COMPANY, }
104 BROADWAY, New York, August 27th, 1869.}

HENRY A. GOUGE, ESQ.—Dear Sir: The ventilating apparatus introduced by you into our office, occupying the large basement of the above named building, does its work perfectly and to our entire satisfaction. Previously, an attempt at ventilation had been made by introducing steam pipes into flues from the basement opening into the atmosphere at the top of the building, with the expectation that the heated pipes would rarify the air in the flues, and thereby cause an ascending current which would carry off the foul air from our office. They were introduced evidently at great expense, and were a total failure.

My own health, and also that of our Secretary and employees, suffered seriously, and the foul and impure atmosphere of our office was a subject of daily remark by our Directors and others visiting us.

Since you introduced your Atmospheric Ventilating Apparatus the air has been sweet and wholesome, and entirely free from bad odors. None of us now suffer from headache, or the lassitude and sickly feeling which always results from breathing foul air. We cheerfully recommend the adoption of your apparatus by others situated as we are.

Yours, etc.,   V. TILYOU, President.

SPECIAL CASES OF VENTILATION.

PRESERVING-ROOM AND DWELLING-HOUSE. — In this connection we take pleasure in referring to A. S. Hatch, Esq., of the firm of Fiske and Hatch, who conduct one of the largest banking-houses in New York City, and who are known all over the commercial world. Ten years ago Mr. Hatch applied to me, through his architect, to build a *Preserving-Room* for him, which was done according to order. With this he was much pleased, and he wished to know whether his dwelling could not be ventilated upon the same principle. This led me to examine his house, which is an elegant structure in Park Avenue, and which I found to be extremely deficient in ventilation, notwithstanding the usual supply of " ventilating flues " in the walls. The parlors were rendered offensive by the odors from the kitchen, while the second and third floors were equally offensive from contiguous water-closets. It need only be stated that those difficulties were entirely removed by the employment of our ventilating apparatus, which was fully appreciated by Mr. Hatch and his family. Instead of the foul odors which had annoyed them so much, they now had a sweet and pleasant atmosphere.

DWELLING-HOUSE — SKEPTICISM — A SEVERE TEST. — We have occasion in this connection to introduce the name of W. B. Hatch, Esq., who is a representative man, and the active partner of Fairbanks and Co., the noted scale manufacturers. He came to me in a skeptical mood to inquire about ventilation, and seemed to be almost angry with himself for condescending to talk upon the subject. He had no faith in any of the theories or systems of ventilation, and considered them all as so many delusions. This stubborn spirit of skepticism we generally consider a good sign, and take pleasure now and then in witnessing its manifestation. Accordingly, we made the best explanations we could to Mr. Hatch, but without changing his views. He could not understand how an insignificant jet of gas, burning in a lantern, connected with a series of air-ducts, could produce the powerful ascensional currents which are necessary for good ventilation. The cause was altogether too slight, in his estimation, for so grand an effect. He left us for the time, proposing to reflect upon the subject. He returned in a few days, and said that his house was much in need of ventilation, but that he was still without faith in our system. We then proposed to ventilate his house, and make no charge for our services unless we succeeded in giving him satisfaction. He accepted our proposition, and we accompanied him to his residence at the corner of Madison Avenue and Forty-Second Street. We found an elegant house sadly deficient in ventilation, which is much too common with the elegant houses of New York City. Some time elapsed, however, before we commenced our labors. The house, meanwhile, had been closed for the summer, the family having gone to the country. The person in charge of it was obliged to open the windows every day or two for the admission of fresh air, which was necessary to prevent the carpets, pictures, and furniture from moulding, or receiving other injury, which they were liable to do from the damp and impure atmosphere of the house.

We proceeded to ventilate the house, which we did on the most extensive scale. Skeptical as we had found Mr. Hatch in our first interviews, he was not disposed to adopt any half-way measures in the proposed ventilation. He ordered us to ventilate the kitchen, parlors, sleeping-rooms, closets, main hall, and last, though not least, the refrigerator. Notwithstanding the house was large, we arranged to accomplish the entire ventilation with only two gas-jets.

Our work being completed, it remained for Mr. Hatch to say whether it was acceptable or otherwise. He proposed a practical but severe test to determine this matter. Instead

of having the doors and windows of the house opened every
day or two for the admission of fresh air, as had been his
custom, he ordered it to be tightly closed for two weeks.
Meanwhile the ventilating apparatus was to be kept in
operation. The weather being warm, he knew very well
that this test would settle the question as to the value of our
ventilation. We had no objection to the test. Indeed, we
solicit exactly such scrutiny as this; and it would be well
for all persons who have resolved to have their houses or
buildings ventilated, to be just as skeptical as Mr. Hatch,
before agreeing to pay out their money.

The two weeks having passed, Mr. Hatch proceeded to
open and examine his house. He went into the kitchen,
the parlors, the sleeping-rooms, and the closets. There was
no part of the interior that did not come under his search-
ing inspection. He hurried from one room to another,
but could find no evidence of a damp or impure atmosphere.
He examined the ventilating apparatus, and found it to be
in operation. He concluded, therefore, that it had been
silently but steadily at work for the previous two weeks,
without any guardian or overseer, conveying away every
particle of the damp, mephitic, or unwholesome vapors and
gases from the interior of the building. After a somewhat
prolonged investigation, he said, very emphatically, "The
atmosphere of my house is as pure as the out-door atmosphere!" Mr. Hatch is now a willing advocate of our system of ventilation, considering it his duty to make known
his convictions to those who may value his opinion upon the
subject.

GLENHAM HOTEL — No SUCCESS, NO PAY — This is a
first-class hotel in Fifth Avenue. We found the kitchen
in a wretched condition, being very hot and very foul. Some
of the cooks had left in consequence, and those that
remained found it difficult to attend to their duties. The
disgusting odors from the kitchen, moreover, had made
their way up in the rear of the house to some of the elegant
rooms above. This, of course, rendered them untenantable,
or, to say the least, impaired their attractiveness for first-
class occupants. A new cooking-range had been put into
the kitchen, and in connection with it a large brick flue had

been constructed, which extended from the kitchen to the top
of the house. This flue, built at great expense, was guaranteed to ventilate the kitchen ; but like all guarantees of the
kind, it amounted to nothing. The hot and foul air of the
kitchen remained ; and, in the veriest despair, not wishing
to have the cooks suffocated, a large hole was made in the
wall which separated the kitchen from the rear yard.
Through this aperture, together with the open doors and
windows, it was hoped to obtain a little fresh air. Under
these peculiar circumstances, the lessees of the house,
Messrs. J. E. Miller and Co., called upon us for our services,
and in consequence of the guarantee mentioned above,
which had proved a snare and a delusion, they wished to
know if we were willing to adhere to our established motto,
" No success, no pay." To this we made no objection, and
proceeded to ventilate the kitchen, in which we were entirely
successful. The atmosphere was rendered cool and pleasant, and the cooks no longer made any complaint. We
also constructed a *Preserving-Room* for the establishment,
which the lessees had discovered was indispensable to a
first-class hotel.

BLOODGOOD AND COMPANY'S BANKING-HOUSE. — This
well-known establishment is at 22 William Street. The
proprietors, Messrs. John Bloodgood and Co., are the treas-
urers of the Peabody Fund, designed for the erection of a
fitting monument to the late George Peabody, Esq. We
found the atmosphere of the place in a horrible condition.
The clerks and officers suffered exceedingly. But this is
an old story which we need hardly repeat. We ventilated
the place, and an immediate change was perceived in the
atmosphere. " It's all right now !" said one of the clerks,
whom Mr. Bloodgood interrogated upon the subject. " It's
an entirely different place !" said another clerk. " We felt
the change at once !" said a third. " All the difference
imaginable !" said a fourth. " It's a pleasure to work here
now !" said a fifth. These were some of the expressions of
the clerks in reference to the atmosphere, after ventilation
had been established. Our bill for the job was $593, which
Mr. Bloodgood said was cheap enough.

UNION TELEGRAPH COMPANY.—This Company was then at 145 Broadway. We ventilated the office, in which we found a close atmosphere, not at all agreeable to the occupants. The well-known President of the Company, William Orton, Esq., in a letter to us, says, "The hall of the first floor of our building, which had become exceedingly offensive from the use of urinals, has been rendered entirely inodorous, and the air kept continually pure therein by the introduction of your Atmospheric Ventilator, with the action of which we are entirely satisfied."

EQUITABLE LIFE ASSURANCE SOCIETY OF THE UNITED STATES.—This well known institution was at No. 92 Broadway, but was soon after removed to the elegant building erected for the purpose at the corner of Cedar Street and Broadway. The Vice-President, H. B. Hyde, Esq., is a member of Dr. Hall's church, on Fifth Avenue, and being pleased with our ventilation of said church, was induced to consult us in relation to the ventilation of the office and rooms of the above Company. He described the atmosphere of the place as being almost suffocating; and although the Company were not to remain in it more than a year, in consequence of the proposed removal to the new building, Mr. Hyde gave me an order to ventilate the office and rooms without delay, as he was unwilling to be exposed any longer to so foul an atmosphere. He also gave me an order to ventilate the new building mentioned above. The result of our ventilation of the old building, etc., is duly set forth in the annexed letter to us, dated December 30, 1868:

H. A. GOUGE, ESQ., New York—Dear Sir: I take great pleasure in giving you my testimony as to the good qualities and performances of your "Atmospheric Ventilator," and have no hesitation in saying that it is the most perfect and serviceable article for the use intended that I have ever seen. Having had recent occasion to examine the various ventilators offered to the public, I speak not entirely at random. Your ventilators are in daily approved use, both at my house and at the office of the Equitable Life Assurance Society of the United States, No. 92 Broadway, New York, where they may be examined by those who desire to secure a pure and healthy atmosphere.   H. B. HYDE.

VENTILATION IN CHICAGO.—In May, 1869, previous to the great fire, we ventilated the Comptroller's office in Chicago, which was then in the Court House. The work was superintended by Mr. W. I. Reid, who was at that time our assistant, and to whom we are mainly indebted for the particulars relating to the work. The building was over-run with rats and cockroaches, rendering the atmosphere extremely offensive. It was found necessary to remove some of the flooring, under which the rats had an abiding place, and the stench emitted from this enclosure was horrible beyond description. The Comptroller's Room, nevertheless, was the most offensive place in the building, which was partly due to its situation over the jail kitchen. So foul and poisonous was its atmosphere, that scarcely a day passed without some one of the employees being obliged to go home in consequence of illness. Mr. Charles C. Chase, the Comptroller's special assistant, is spoken of as having suffered more than any one else from the foul atmosphere. Nausea and headache were his leading troubles. After ven-tilation was established, he told Mr. Reid, with great appar-ent pleasure, that these troubles had entirely ceased, and that, in consequence of his improved health, he was enabled to extend his labors into the night, which, previously, he had found to be impossible. The City Comptroller's endorsement will be found among our Testimonials.

CHURCH VENTILATION.

THE CHRISTIAN CHURCH.—This is a handsome edifice in Twenty-Eighth Street, near Broadway. Like most of the churches, it was poorly ventilated. The atmosphere was very close and disagreeable. One of the leading members of the church, referring to the bad atmosphere, remarked— "Although we have a brilliant and eloquent preacher, it is impossible, in this sleepy and confined air, for many of his hearers to keep awake during the services."

P. B. Roberts, Esq., who is a well-known citizen of New York, was one of the trustees of the church, and was appointed to make inquiries in reference to its ventilation. It happened that we had constructed a *Preserving-Room* for him, a year or two previously, at his residence in Fifth Avenue, with which he was pleased, and he naturally sought us out in reference to ventilating the Christian Church. I examined the building at his request, and found that various experiments had been made with a view to its ventilation, but without success. One experiment consisted of openings in the ceiling, which were to convey the stagnant air of the church into the general space between the ceiling and the roof, passing ultimately through openings in the roof, terminated by tubular caps. Another experiment had relation to the large chandelier in the dome of the church. Tubes connected with the gas-jets of the chandelier were made to pass through the ceiling above into the open space already indicated, and then through the capped orifices in the roof. This, we believe, is a French device, but does not seem to answer a good purpose.

I furnished a plan to Mr. Roberts for the ventilation of the church, which he accepted upon condition that I would make no charge for my work unless it proved successful. I proceeded, accordingly, to ventilate the church, and, in connection with it, a number of other rooms, used for lectures, Sunday-school, prayer meetings, etc. My bill for the entire work was $1,575, for which I promptly received a check, showing that the ventilation was satisfactory to Mr. Roberts and those whom he represented.

CALVARY BAPTIST CHURCH—NATHAN BISHOP, LL. D.— This church is in Twenty-Third Street, between Fifth and Sixth Avenues. The school-rooms connected with it were damp and unhealthy. On this account we were applied to for our services by Dr. Nathan Bishop, a distinguished scholar, whose name holds a prominent place among our Testimonials, and who was a member of the church. We ventilated the rooms in question, and relieved them of the damp and unhealthy atmosphere.

DR. HALL'S CHURCH—A RIGID CONTRACT—CHURCH-HEADACHE, ETC.—This church was at the corner of Fifth Avenue and Nineteenth Street. Dr. Hall is very popular, and is attracting large and fashionable audiences. He preached in Dublin, Ireland, before coming to this country, where he was also popular. The close atmosphere of the church, due to the crowds of people assembling there, was a subject of general complaint. Some of the leading members were almost unwilling to attend the services in consequence of suffering with headache, which is one of the usual concomitants of foul air. Various popular devices for ventilating the church had been tried, some of which we will briefly notice. Apertures had been made in the ceiling for the escape of the foul air, but, as usual, it would not make its escape. Side and end windows, with traps, so as to be opened or closed at will, had been employed, but they proved to be worthless. At length the Board of Trustees applied to me, asking whether I could give them any relief. I proposed to ventilate the church, and make no charge for my labors unless I should prove successful. To this the trustees assented, and a lawyer was selected to draft an article of agreement, setting forth that I was to ventilate the church aforesaid, including the lecture-room and school-room, and render each and all of them free from noxious gases, and other atmospheric impurities, or have no legal claim upon the church for payment. It was further provided that the trustees should have a certain definite time to test the ventilation, and in case it should not prove satisfactory to them, a committee of investigation was to be appointed to decide the questions at issue, determining whether I should receive the full amount of my bill, or only a part of the same, or whether indeed I should receive anything at all. In case it should be decided by the committee that my ventilating apparatus had no value, it was provided that I should remove said apparatus at my own expense, and leave the church-building in the same good condition in which I found it.

This legal document was duly executed, and, in accordance with its provisions, I proceeded to ventilate the church, having voluntarily placed myself at the mercy of the trustees. If the reader should inquire why so rigid a contract was proposed by the trustees, he may be reminded that exorbitant sums of money have been occasionally paid for experiments in ventilation which proved to be utter failures; and it has further happened, in some instances, that additional sums of money had to be expended in removing the worthless apparatus and putting the house or building into its previous good condition. It is entirely proper, therefore, that our citizens should protect themselves against contingencies of this unfortunate character. If less confidence had been reposed in adventurous but plausible experimenters in ventilation, we would have less trouble in commending ourself to the favor and appreciation of a generous public.

When the ventilation of the church was completed, a rigid investigation was entered into, and a noted chemist was employed to give his opinion in relation to the motive power which we employ in our system of ventilation. We have not this document at hand, and therefore do not know whether the opinions of the chemist were favorable or unfavorable. We are happy to say, however, that after a full investigation of the subject, our bill, amounting to $2,700, was paid in full, which is a sufficient indication that our work received the sanction of the Board of Trustees.

Among the prominent members of the church who have signified their approval of the ventilation, we will venture to name William Paton, then of the firm of Paton and Co., 311 Broadway, extensive linen importers; Parker Handy, then Vice-President of the Third National Bank, and H. B. Hyde, Esq., now President of the Equitable Life Assurance Society of the United States.

As an evidence of Mr. Hyde's appreciation, he employed us to ventilate the office and rooms now occupied by the above Life Assurance Society, as well as the new and elegant building at the corner of Cedar Street and Broadway,

Mr. Paton's testimony in regard to the ventilation is interesting. He is devoid of the sense of smell, which physicians tell us is no uncommon thing, and was incapable, therefore, of detecting any unpleasant odor in the atmosphere of the church through this important sense. Nevertheless, he was always advised of a foul atmosphere in the church by the recurrence of a headache, which would manifest itself soon after taking his seat. It is interesting to know that he has had none of this headache since the church was ventilated. It matters not whether he sits in the body of the church, or in either of the galleries, he is equally free from suffering. This indicates that the ventilation is equally good throughout the whole interior of the church. This *church-headache*, therefore, as it may be properly termed, is clearly the result of foul air, and the discovery is important, inasmuch as physicians tell us that we must first ascertain the cause of a disease before we can be successful in applying a remedy. In Mr. Paton's case, therefore, and in hundreds of similar cases, the remedy is ventilation;

VENTILATION OF SCHOOL ROOMS.

Nobody needs to be reminded of the celebrity of the Grammar School founded in New York by the late Prof. Anthon; a name widely known in connection with the history of Columbia College, and with the Latin and Greek classics. Well aware that ventilation had hitherto been a matter of pure theory without performance, and feeling no assurance that it would or could be really effected, this gentleman applied to us to know if we would submit to the extreme test of agreeing to put in and take out our work at our own expense in case the prescribed quantity of air per minute should prove not to be regularly changed, by measure. We had no hesitation, and took no risk whatever, in agreeing to this contract.

This is what he says of the result:

VENTILATION OF THE ANTHON GRAMMAR SCHOOL.

252 Madison Ave., N. Y., Jan. 11, 1872.

In October, 1871, Mr. Henry A. Gouge was directed by me to introduce his system of ventilation into the buildings now occupied by this school. He was not limited as to expense, nor interfered with in any way, and the result is all I can desire.

I can discover no difference between the air in the halls and that in the rooms, where classes of thirty boys have been sitting with closed doors for an hour or more.

Mr. Gouge introduced three distinct shafts, each carrying off the foul air from four rooms. About four hundred cubic feet a minute is discharged from each room. I hear no more complaints of headache from my pupils, and see no flushed faces when I enter the class rooms. The boys work with more vigor, and my twelve teachers and one hundred and fifty pupils are unanimous in the expression of their satisfaction.

GEO C. ANTHON.

Four years later, March 10, 1875, Prof. Anthon wrote us again, fully confirming the above statements to date. He added that he had found it the best investment he had ever made, both for the efficiency and for the popularity of his school.

FEMALE SEMINARY VENTILATED.

Among the Young Ladies' Seminaries patronized by the wealthy citizens of New York, that of Miss Anna C. Brackett stands pre-eminent. This lady reckons among the causes of her brilliant success, the pure and vitalizing atmosphere in which her teachers and pupils have pursued their labors since our ventilating apparatus was introduced.

Following is her statement:

9 West 39th Street, New York City, March 8th, 1875.

Mr. H. A. Gouge,

Dear Sir,—The two ventilating shafts which you put into this house last fall, and which have been in full operation since Dec. 10th, 1874, have worked to our perfect satisfaction.

With our seventy pupils in rooms not originally designed for school purposes, all through the days of winter, with all the doors and windows closed, there has never been any time when the air seemed in the least impure. In addition to this fact, we have not, during the whole time, been aware by any odor that any cooking was going on in the house, though the kitchen is in the basement, and three meals a day for twenty persons are prepared. Among the eleven young ladies whom I have had in my family, I have had during the winter almost no complaint of headache. The whole school has borne witness to the fact that the air was not becoming vitiated by being as attentive in their last recitation as in their first, and the air seems perfectly pure when they leave the rooms at 2 p. m., after having been in them since 9 a. m.

ANNA C. BRACKETT.

PUBLIC SCHOOLS.

Public schools also in some of the suburban cities, such as Brooklyn and Yonkers, have been ventilated to the satisfaction of the most captious and incredulous of committees and official architects. It could not be otherwise, for the prescribed criterion was the measurement of the air passing each register every minute, in cubic feet, by a scientific instrument that cannot be contradicted, that indulges in no guesswork, and that tells no lies.

VENTILATION OF BOSTON PUBLIC SCHOOLS.

We have elsewhere stated how it is that the public schools of New York remain unventilated, and have fully shown what a disgrace to civilization their actual condition has always been and still remains. In Boston, however, we are happy to report that a different spirit and state of things exists. We have ventilated a number of their model schools during the last ten years, and our work had no careless or accommodating inspection to meet. One school in particular, attended by some 500 children of the tenement-house population, was a severe test ; and yet not any more difficult or doubtful, for us, than those in the most refined quarters of the city. The only difference was that we decided to give them full hospital supply : that is, to take out twenty cubic feet of air per minute for every person, and replace it with fresh air at the same rate. Not that these children needed or consumed any more oxygen than the better dressed and washed : but we were determined also to remove all offensive odors and exhalations, and make the room pleasant to the senses as well as salubrious,—and we did it. There were eight large school rooms with sixty scholars in each, and we set 1,200 cubic feet of air going out of each of those rooms per minute, and 1,200 cubic feet of fresh air coming in, in such a manner that it has been going out and coming in at that rate every minute to the present time, if the apparatus has not been neglected or damaged. When the Superintendent, the architect, the Trustees and the doctors came together to inspect the result and decide whether we had duly executed our contract, the movement of air was critically measured. Dr. Draper and Dr. Nichols, with the rest, measured the currents at all the registers with their anemometer, and we measured them with our own. The 9,600 feet were unanimously found and attested, and it is remarkable that there was not more than ten feet difference between their measure and ours.

TESTIMONIALS.

VENTILATION OF THE HOWARD MISSION.

264 and 266 Canal Street, New York, Jan. 15, 1872.

H. A. Gouge, Esq. :

Dear Sir, —The question of ventilation has been for a long time under consideration by the Board of Managers at the Howard Mission, 40 New Bowery. Various methods have been proposed and discarded, and I must confess that when your plan of ventilation was proposed I had very great misgivings as to its utility, but after a very thorough examination it was adopted, and I now have very great pleasure in certifying that, after using it for several months, we find it ventilates the rooms thoroughly, and is entirely satisfactory.

Yours, very truly,

WM. PHELPS, Treas.

VENTILATION OF COLUMBIA COLLEGE LAW SCHOOL.

New York, January 16th, 1872.

My Dear Sir,—I take pleasure in stating my views of the Ventilating Apparatus placed by you in the building occupied by this Law School.

Our building is not very well adapted to our purposes, and our principal lecture room crowded with students. When your Ventilator is not in operation I perceive it in my own feelings at once. The air is oppressive, and there is a general langour about me. The students perceptibly lose their interest in the exercises. When the Ventilator is in full operation, with a connection with the outer air, all is changed. I would not be without it in winter for any consideration. It is not so essential in summer, as we have good ventilation by three large windows.

I hope you will prosper in your most useful work.

Yours, sincerely,

THEODORE W. DWIGHT, Prof. of Law, &c.

H. A. Gouge, Esq.

VENTILATION OF GILMAN & SON'S BANKING HOUSE.

Gilman, Son & Co., New York, Jan. 16th, 1872.

H. A. Gouge, Esq.:

Dear Sir,—Your Ventilating Apparatus has been in operation for about four years in our office, and has relieved us from an unhealthy state of atmosphere from which we suffered before its introduction.

We know of no apparatus which accomplishes a like result, and we would not be without ours.

Where your system has been introduced we have never heard of complaints of its ill success.

We are, very truly,

GILMAN, SON & CO.

I fully concur in the above.

JAMES WINSLOW, V. P. Third N. Bk.

VENTILATION OF DREXEL, MORGAN & CO'S. BANKING HOUSE.

53 Exchange Place, N. Y., Jan. 18th, 1872.

Henry A. Gouge, Esq.:

Dear Sir,—We take pleasure in stating that your Ventilating Apparatus which has been in use in our office nearly four months gives complete satisfaction.

We were previously greatly troubled with foul air, from which the use of several devices had not relieved us. There is now no cause for complaint of that kind, all in our office uniting in the opinion that your Apparatus is entirely effectual.

Yours, very truly,

DREXEL, MORGAN & CO.

VENTILATION OF FISK & HATCH'S BANKING HOUSE.

Fisk & Hatch, Bankers, New York, Jan. 24, 1872.

To Whom it may Concern:

Having personally and intimately known Mr. H. A. Gouge for a number of years, I take very great pleasure in commending him to the courtesy and confidence of all with whom my esteem and good opinion may have any weight.

I have been for some time more or less familiar with the principles and the practical workings of his system of ventilation, and have had personal experience of its efficiency in my own dwelling house, and in a public institution with which I am connected. I have no hesitation in expressing my unqualified opinion that it is superior to any other plan of ventilation of which I have any knowledge, so far as my experience of it enables me to judge.

Very respectfully,

A. S. HATCH.

VENTILATION OF IMPORTERS' AND TRADERS' BANK.

Importers' & Traders' Bank, New York, Nov. 20, 1873.

Mess. H. A. Gouge & Co., New York:

Dear Sir,—Your arrangement for ventilating this Bank has been in use about two years, and we can say with much pleasure that it has worked very satisfactorily, and proved itself all you claimed for it. It has been a great blessing to us all, and we would hardly be willing to do without it.

Respectfully yours,

E. H. PERKINS, Jr., Cashier.

VENTILATION OF THE CHEMICAL NATIONAL BANK.

Chemical National Bank, New York, Dec. 29, 1873.

We have had in operation in our banking room, for a period of about two years, Gouge's System of Ventilation, and have found the same serviceable in the highest degree.

With a corps of about thirty clerks, and numerous dealers constantly coming and going, and a number of gas burners lighted a good part of the time, we found some ventilation essential; and have every reason to be satisfied with the system adopted, and take pleasure in commending it highly to all having similar need of relief from the deleterious influences of foul air.

G. G. WILLIAMS, Cashier.

VENTILATION OF THE MERCANTILE NATIONAL BANK, NEW YORK.

Mercantile National Bank, New York, Jan. 24, 1874.

Mess. H. A. Gouge & Co.,

Gentlemen,—Your Ventilating Apparatus has given entire satisfaction here, and its beneficial effect is appreciated by every one in our office. We can, with confidence, recommend its introduction to any one who has the matter under consideration.

Yours very truly,

N. AMERMAN, Cashier.

VENTILATION OF THE FIRST NATIONAL BANK, NEW YORK.

New York, March 17, 1875.

H. A. Gouge, Esq.,

Dear Sir,—In response to your inquiry we reply that our room, containing over forty clerks, and as many gas burners, we found impracticable to ventilate with any degree of comfort, until we tried your system, which gives great satisfaction.

Yours respectfully.

GEO. F. BAKER, Cashier.

VENTILATION OF THE MUTUAL LIFE INSURANCE COMPANY.

The Mutual Life Ins. Co. of N. Y., 144 & 146 B'way, Nov. 16, 1874.

Mr. H. A. Gouge:

Your efforts to improve the ventilation of the rooms in the actuarial department of this Company have been successful, and I very cheerfully commend your plans to others suffering, as we did, from the effects of bad air.

Yours very truly,

WM. H. C. BARTLETT.

VENTILATION OF THE EQUITABLE BUILDING AND PRESIDENT'S HOUSE.

Equitable Life Assurance Soc'y, December 16th, 1873.

Mess. H. A. Gouge & Co.:

Gentlemen,—I take pleasure in bearing testimony to the excellence of your work, and the highly satisfactory Ventilation, which is the result of your system.

The work done under your supervision in our offices, and in my house, has been very effective, and is strongly in contrast with the failures of others who have preceded you.

I regret that we did not avail ourselves of your services in the beginning, as our offices were constructed in accordance with the plans of other parties, and the arrangements made were so unsatisfactory that, after various unsuccessful experiments, the result arrived at was only reached after radical changes had been made by you.

Yours truly,

H. B. HYDE, V. P.

EQUITABLE LIFE ASSURANCE SOCIETY—FURTHER TESTIMONY OF H. B. HYDE, ESQ.

April 1st, 1875.

H. A. Gouge, Esq., New York,

My Dear Sir,—It gives me great pleasure to express my continued satisfaction with your system of Ventilation, which has done constant and effective service for several years past, in the Equitable Life Assurance Building, New York. My experience of the practical use of your plan enables me to speak confidently of its many advantages over other appliances.

Very truly yours,

H. B. HYDE, President.

FROM DEPARTMENT OF CITY WORKS, BROOKLYN—OFFICE VENTILATED.

Department of City Works, Commissioners' Office.
Brooklyn, March 15th, 1875.

Mess. H. A. Gouge & Co.

Gentlemen,—I wish you could convince some of our city officials, and the rest of mankind, of the true merits of your system of Ventilation. It has worked so remarkably well in our office, that it seems to be almost a missionary's duty to advocate it as a true system. When any person of intelligence examines into its merits you are sure of a convert.

Respectfully yours,

LORIN PALMER, President.

PHELPS, DODGE & CO.—HOUSE AND STABLE VENTILATED.

Phelps, Dodge & Co., July 8th, 1873.

H. A. Gouge, Esq.:

Dear Sir,—I have had my house and stable ventilated by your system for some years. The plan seems simple, direct and effective. It has worked much better than I anticipated, and given me great satisfaction.

Yours respectfully,

W. E. DODGE, Jr.

FROM ALEX. M. HAYS & CO.—STORE VENTILATED.

23 Maiden Lane, New York, March 19, 1875.

H. A. Gouge, Esq.,

Dear Sir,—Your letter of inquiry requesting my opinion of your patent Ventilator is received. In reply, would state that, after a thorough and lengthened trial of the same, I am thoroughly satisfied of its efficacy.

For years my store was filled with a most disagreeable and unhealthy air, which your Ventilator has entirely removed.

I am, sir, very truly yours,

ALEX. M. HAYS, Prop.

H. B. Claflin & Co., New York, Nov. 12, 1874.

Henry A. Gouge, Esq.,
Dear Sir,—Your invention is a success. Everyone in the office notices the improvement of the ventilation, and we no longer hear complaints of semi-suffocation.
We think the life companies owe you many thanks.
Yours truly,
H. B. CLAFLIN & CO.

Mercantile Mutual Ins. Co., New York, Jan. 23, 1874.

Henry A. Gouge, Esq.,
Dear Sir,—It gives us great pleasure to accord to you the credit of having by your process of Ventilation thoroughly purified the atmosphere of our offices, at the same time affording the means of keeping the temperature at an even point.
We cheerfully recommend your system of Ventilation to all who require anything of the kind, as we sincerely think it is the best in use.
Yours very respectfully,
ELLWOOD WALTER, Pres't.

Methodist Book Concern, New York, July 9, 1874.

It gives us great pleasure to say that Mr. Henry A. Gouge, of this City, has put into our building, corner of Broadway and 11th Street, his Ventilating Apparatus, and that having thoroughly tested it, it proves efficient and entirely satisfactory. We are satisfied that Mr. Gouge thoroughly understands Ventilating, and will accomplish whatever he undertakes in that respect.
NELSON & PHILLIPS, Agents for Meth. Bk. Con.

Erie Railway Company, New York, Jan. 31, 1874.

Mess. H. A. Gouge & Co.,
Gentlemen,—The system of ventilation introduced by you in the building occupied by the general offices of this Company, has now been in operation six months, and has accomplished successfully all that was agreed to be executed in your contract.
Prior to its introduction there was universal complaint of the foulness of the air in the offices after they had been occupied any length of time, and at all times, but particularly in winter, the water closets were very offensive. Headaches and other disorders due to foul air, were common among the officers and employees who were confined to the office throughout the day, and there was no means of obtaining a supply of fresh air except by the opening of windows or doors.
This winter I have not heard a complaint of such troubles, and I can say from personal experience that the contrast between the purity of the air in the building this winter, and its closeness, and ofttimes oppressive offensiveness last winter, is most marked.
The water closets are no longer objectionable. I have given the subject of the ventilation of this building considerable attention; and I do not hesitate to say that you have succeeded in giving us plenty of fresh, pure warm air, and entirely corrected the evils under which we suffered previously for the want of this article.
I remain respectfully yours,
GEO. T. BALCH, Gen'l Storekeeper.
Late Engineer in charge of Grand Opera House.

CRUMP LABEL PRESS—OFFICE VENTILATED.

75 Fulton St., New York, April 1st, 1875.

H. A. Gouge, Esq.,

Dear Sir,—Your Ventilating Apparatus, in the opinion of the writer, is the only one on the market that is free from "art and mystery." It takes out the air with all the certainty of a powerful steam fan—costs nothing of consequence to operate, and will last a life time.

Respectfully,

SAMUEL CRUMP.

HOTELS.

ALBEMARLE HOTEL, cor. of Fifth Ave. and Twenty-fourth St., New York.

You ask me to say what I think about the Atmospheric Refrigerator. I have used both the Meat-House and Chest for the last ten months. It works beautifully, and to my entire satisfaction. In fact, it comes fully up to your recommendation. I believe it is the only right principle for a Refrigerator.

GEORGE D. IVES, *Proprietor.*

BREVOORT HOUSE, New York, Jan. 19, 1864.

Dear Sir : I have had in use your system of ventilating Meat-Chests and Ice-Houses for eight or ten months, and am so much pleased with its operation that I take every opportunity to show and recommend it to my friends, as being the best thing I know of to preserve meats, with the least quantity of ice.

ALBERT CLARK, *Proprietor.*

ST. NICHOLAS HOTEL, N. Y., Jan. 21, 1864.

Dear Sir : We are well satisfied with our experience that your mode of ventilating Meat-Houses is a decided improvement, and will commend itself for its good preserving qualities and saving of ice, to all who test it properly.

Yours truly, SPOTTS & HAWK.

FIFTH AVE. HOTEL, New York, Feb. 2, 1865.

Mr. H. A. GOUGE : Dear Sir—We take pleasure in assuring you that after a long and thorough trial of your Ventilating Apparatus, we are convinced that it is the very best of the kind extant. Very truly yours,

HITCHCOCK, DARLING & CO.

ST. JAMES HOTEL, New York, Jan. 19, 1864.

Dear Sir : Having thoroughly tested your patent Ice-House, constructed for this hotel, we cheerfully add our testimony to the many testimonials in its praise, as being, in our opinion, the most perfect and economical of those now in use. It not only preserves the meats, etc., for an indefinite time, but it consumes very little ice. Wishing you every success, we remain,

Very respectfully yours, T. F. WELLS & CO., *Proprietors.*

BRANDETH HOUSE, New York, Jan. 20, 1864.

Dear Sir : We take great pleasure in certifying that we have had in use for nearly a year one of your Ice-Houses, erected by you, and which has given us entire satisfaction. We find it to keep Meats, Fish, etc., with the use of a small quantity of ice ; and think it the most economical thing of the kind that can be used in a hotel. Yours very truly, J. CURTIS & CO.

172

MERCHANTS' HOTEL, 41 Cortlandt Street, N. Y., May 8, 1865.
Dear Sir: We have had in use the large Meat-House you constructed for this Hotel now about one year; it has given us entire satisfaction. The ventilation seems to be perfect.   Yours, etc.,
                                        CLARKE & SCHENCK.

WESTERN HOTEL, 9 Cortlandt Street, N. Y., May 6, 1865.
Dear Sir: The Atmospheric Meat-House which you constructed for this hotel has now been in use for about one year, and has given entire satisfaction. I know of no other system of Ventilating which is effectual; your plan appears as perfect as it is simple.   D. D. WINCHESTER.

BELMONT HOTEL, 133 to 137 Fulton St., N. Y., May 9, 1865.
Mr. H. A. GOUGE: Dear Sir—The Ventilating Apparatus put up by you in my dining-room about four months ago is a complete success. I am very much pleased with its operation. The room has been greatly improved by it. The principle is undoubtedly correct. Yours respectfully,   J. P. RICHARDS.

PRIVATE HOUSES.

This certifies that I have used your Atmospheric Refrigerator during the last nine months, and I can truly say that it surpasses all methods that have been in use for preserving in an edible condition whatever may be placed within it. In fact, I believe it comes fully up to the claims of the inventor.
SAM'L S. GUY, M.D., 181 Fort Greene Place, Brooklyn, N.Y.

The Refrigerator you sent me last season has proved to be all you claim for it. I think it surpasses your modest recommendations as the correct method for preserving Meat and Fish, (raw and cooked), Fruit and Vegetables; and I have no doubt but you will find that this will soon supersede all other Refrigerators in use.   WILLIAM H. SMITH, 42 West Jersey St., Elizabeth, N. J.

I take pleasure in recommending your improved principle for Refrigerators, as the most scientific and perfect yet offered to the public. The one which you introduced into my house about a year ago has never failed to accomplish all that you promised for it.   Yours,
                    JOHN D. ASCOUGH, 171 West 11th St., New York.

We have used the Atmospheric Refrigerator in our family for the last year. I believe it to be the best Refrigerator in the world, and I can't conceive how it can be more perfect. We place all articles of food in it with Sweet Butter, etc., and we have none of the experience that I have had with other Refrigerators. You have conceived a plan that will surpass all others, without doubt.
Yours,   JOSEPH SCOTT, Silver Plater.
No. 70 John St., New York, and 24 Butler St., Brooklyn.

PROVISION HOUSES.

Mr. H. A. GOUGE: The Ventilating Apparatus you put up for me works to my entire satisfaction. I think I have given it as severe a test as it can be possibly put to. My cooling-rooms (25 x 50) which were in my cellar and sub-cellar, were in a very bad condition—foul and damp—so much so it was very unhealthy for men, water constantly dropping from the ceiling. Since I have had your Apparatus there are no signs of dampness; the atmosphere is perfectly dry and pure; have not had a man complain of sickness. My pork cures as well in summer as in a winter atmosphere of 38 or 39 degrees. Your invention has been very valuable to me, and I cheerfully recommend it to Pork Packers, Butchers, etc., as the best thing I am acquainted with for the purpose.
HENRY SILVERHORN, Pork Packer, 92 Christie St., N. Y.

173

NEW YORK, 152 West Street, Jan. 31, 1864.

Mr. H. A. GOUGE: Dear Sir—Some few months ago we were at a loss to know what kind of an Ice House to put in our Packing House, which we were then fitting up, when you came to us and proposed to put up your Ventilating Chill Rooms, and not to charge us a cent if they did not work well. We are happy to say that they did all you claimed for them, to our perfect satisfaction. A cold, dry, pure air, such as cannot be got in any other ice house.

Yours truly,
D. & W. H. MILLEMAN, 152 West Street.

BROOKLYN, New York, Jan. 29, 1864.

Dear Sir: About one year ago, as an experiment, we had your Ventilating Apparatus applied to one of our Cooling Rooms, at our Packing House in Raymond Street. We are now satisfied with its utility enough to have it applied to all of our rooms. We believe it makes a perfect ventilation.

Very respectfully,   JOSEPH LOCKITT & CO.

BUTCHERS' MEAT HOUSES.

NEW-YORK, Jan. 27, 1864.

Dear Sir: I have had in use the Atmospheric Meat House you built for me, now about one year, through an unusually hot summer, and ice of the poorest quality. I can say that it has given me entire satisfaction, and, as I tell my friends, I never paid for any thing that gave me so much real pleasure. I cheerfully recommend it to butchers and families as the best Refrigerator that I am acquainted with.   Yours, etc.,

DAN'L F. FERNALD.
Union Market, Tillary, cor. Fulton St., Brooklyn, New York.

The Meat House you built for me last June suits me in every particular. The ventilation is so perfect, the air within is always perfectly pure and dry, free from sweat or moisture of any kind. I can hang meat up in this house with the animal heat in it, and it will cure as perfectly as in a winter atmosphere of 38 to 40 degrees. With my experience, I conceive it to be the most useful invention of the age for the purpose. I cheerfully recommend it to the trade generally.   Wishing you every success, yours respectfully

CHARLES W. CONWAY, Butcher, 275 3d Ave., N. Y.

This is to certify that I have used in my business the Atmospheric Mea House for the last nine months, and will say that it works to my entire satisfac tion, both summer and winter. I have experimented with it, particularly as to its quality of preserving Fruit, and am satisfied for this purpose it can't be beat. I believe this Meat House is the best thing ever used for the purpose.

D. TILTON, Dealer in Poultry and Game,
No. 12 Franklin Market, and 74 & 76 Tompkins Market, New York.

444 SIXTH AVENUE, New York, Jan. 23, 1864.

Dear Sir: I have great pleasure in bearing testimony to the very superior system adopted by you of ventilating Meat Chests and Ice Houses. I have now tried your plan some time, and it gives me great satisfaction in saying that it is far superior to any others, and I shall consider it to be my duty to recommend its adoption to my friends.   I am, dear sir, yours respectfully,

JOSEPH COLWELL.

May 6, 1865.

MR. H. A. GOUGE: Dear Sir—The Ventilating Apparatus put up by you in my shop about one year ago is a complete success; I have kept Meats in it during the summer months for four weeks without taint or change of color, and did not lose a pound of meat during the entire season. I would not do without it for ten times its cost.   B. JOACHIM, 48 Greenwich Street, N.Y.

174

REFERENCES.

SEE TESTIMONIALS FOLLOWING REFERENCES.

HITCHCOCK, DARLING & CO.,.........................Fifth Avenue Hotel, New York.
ALBERT CLARK, Esq.,..........................Proprietor Brevoort House, "
PARAN STEVENS, Esq.,..................................244 Fifth Avenue, "
S. H. GAY, Esq., ...Editor of *New York Tribune.*
J. A. HAMILTON, Esq.,..............................46 Exchange Place, New York.
A. B. DARLING, Esq.,.........................40 West 23d Street, "
SAMUEL SINCLAIR, Esq.,............................Publisher of *New York Tribune.*
Mrs. G. S. ROBBINS,..........................No. 17 West Seventeenth Street, New York.
JAMES H. BANKER, Esq.,...........................President Bank of New York.
Hon. Judge HENRY HILTON......................222 Madison Avenue, "
DANIEL DEVLIN, Esq.,.............................City Chamberlain, "
Hon. WM. DENNISON,....................Postmaster-General, Washington City.
GEORGE RIGGS, Esq.,..................................Banker, "
JAY COOKE & CO.,.....................................Bankers.
Hon. S. J. BOWEN,.................Formerly Postmaster, now Mayor of Washington City.
THOMAS McELRATH, Esq.,...................8 Washington Place, New York.
BREEDEN & SOUTHWICK,.........................109 Liberty Street, "
JOHN MACMULLEN, Esq.,.........Private School for Boys, No. 900 Broadway, "
S. D. BABCOCK, Esq.,................Firm of Babcock Brothers, Bankers, "
MARTIN BATES, Esq.,.................................51 Broadway, "
CHARLES A. MEIGS, Esq.,........................Banker, Exchange Place, "
JAMES S. ELTON, Esq.,.............Secretary Waterbury Brass Co., Waterbury, Conn.
EDWARD SHULZE, Esq.,..........................No. 23 William Street, New York.
LYMAN FISK, Esq.,..................................Stevens House, "
A. McKINNEY, Esq.,..............................121 Beacon Street, Boston.
J. P. RICHARDS, Esq.,.............................Belmont Hotel, New York.
Capt. R. W. MEADE,.................United States Navy, Washington, D. C.
D. D. WINCHESTER, Esq.,.......................Western Hotel, New York.
CLARK & SCHENCK,.............................Merchants' Hotel, "
JOHN W. RITCH, Esq.,......................Architect, 153 Broadway, "
WM. FIELD & SON,.......................Architects, 54 Wall Street, "
WILLIAM B. DITMARS, Esq.,.............Architect, 18 South 7th Street, Brooklyn.
CHARLES COOPER, Esq.,.........................Fulton Market, New York.
CHARLES SCHEDLER, Esq.,.....................24 Broad Street, "
COURT HOUSE, COUNTY OF ESSEX........................Newark, New Jersey.
ADOLPH HAMPE, Esq.,.............................6 Hanover Street, New York.
CLARK & SON,......................................115 Washington Street, "
B. CASSERLY, Esq.,......General Superintendent Commissioners of Emigration, "
McPHERSON SMITH & }
DONALD SMITH, Esqs., }........................Brewers, 160 West 18th Street, "
JAMES E. COULTER, Esq.,..........................Warden City Prison, "
ELIE CHARLIER, Esq.,................Charlier Institute, 24th Street, "
Rev. S. A. FARRAND..................................695 Sixth Avenue, "
E. V. HAUGHWOUT, Esq., ...Cor. Broome and Broadway, "
SAMUEL RAYNOR & CO.,.................Nos. 115 & 117 William Street, "
JOHN HAYS, Esq., Chairman Warming & Ventilating Com., Board of Education, "
Major-Gen. O. O. HOWARD, U. S. A..................... Washington, D.C.
P. ROESSLE & SON,.....................Proprietors Delevan House, Albany.
RITCH & GRIFFITHS,...........................Architects, 153 Broadway, New York.
ROBERT S. HONE, Esq.,.............President Republic Insurance Company, "
HORACE H. DAY, Esq.,.............................23 Cortlandt Street, "
Hon. HORACE GREELEY,.................Editor *New York Tribune,* "

EDWARD CARY, Esq.,..Editor *Brooklyn Union.*
SPRINGFIELD SAVINGS BANK,......................................Springfield, Mass.
DAVIS & CO.,................................Cor. Walker Street & Broadway, New York.
PLYMOUTH SABBATH SCHOOL ROOM (Henry Ward Beecher's),.............Brooklyn.
R. W. RAYMOND, Esq.,..............Superintendent Plymouth Sabbath School,   "
JOHN G. LATIMER, Esq.,.... ....Proprietor of Latimer's Hall,   "
WM. B. JONES, Esq., Supt. Lafayette Av. Mission (Dr. Cuyler's), Cumberland St.,   *
P. B. ROBERTS, Esq.,....................................228 Fifth Avenue, New York.
BRIGADIER-GEN. C. H. HOWARD, U. S. A.,........ ....Washington, D. C.
B. B. FRENCH, Esq.,.................Commissioner of Public Buildings,   "
H. D. COOK, Esq.,.............................Firm of Jay Cook & Co.,   "
ISAAC BELL, Esq.,.......Prest. Commission of Public Charities and Correction, New York.
JOHN E. WILLIAMS, Esq.,....................President Metropolitan Bank,   "
A. V. STOUT, Esq.,...............................President Shoe and Leather Bank   "
BENJAMIN R. WINTHROP, Esq,..........President Deaf and Dumb Asylum,   "
H. W. MEEKER, Esq.,....................Cashier of Bank of New York,   "
C. H. LOUTREL, Esq.,............Firm of Francis & Loutrel, 45 Maiden Lane,   "
NATHAN BISHOP, LL.D.,..11 East 24th Street,   "
ROBERT HOE & CO.,..29 Gold Street,   "
ROBERT HOE, JR., Esq.,... ....43 West 32d Street,   "
PETER S. HOE, Esq.,.............Firm of Robert Hoe & Co., 29 Gold Street,   "
JOHN DUNHAM, Esq.,....................Engineer of the Board of Education,   "
W. E. DODGE, Esq.,.................Firm of Phelps, Dodge & Co., Cliff Street,   "
CALVARY BAPTIST CHURCH,....................No. 5 West 23d Street,   "
MONROE STREET PRESBYTERIAN CHURCH,..............................Brooklyn.
JOHN HOUSTON, Esq.,........ .. ..Engineer, Erie Railroad, New York.
C. E. DOUGLASS,............................170 Fifth Avenue, cor. 22d Street,   "
DENNISTOUN & CO.,......................Bankers, No. 18 Exchange Place,   "
ACKERT & QUICK,...................... ....Builders, Yonkers,   "
FISK & HATCH,...............................Bankers, No. 5 Nassau Street,   "
WM. H. JACKSON & CO.,..Union Square,   "
SPOTTS & HAWK,....................................St. Nicholas Hotel,   "
D. C. SELLER, Esq., Firm of Messrs. Dennistoun & Co., No. 18 Exchange Place,   "
SAMUEL D. BROOKS, M.D.,.......Supt. and Physician N. Y. Juvenile Asylum,   "
GRIFFITH THOMAS, Esq........................Architect, No. 470 Broadway,   "
MOSHER & REED,...... ....St. Denis Hotel,   "
C. H. CHEEVER, Esq.,...89 Fifth Avenue,   "
WALTER BROWN, Esq.,...Newburgh,   "
CAPE, CULVER & CO.,...........................Nos. 16 & 18 Leonard Street,   "
F. A. FERRIS & CO.,. ....No. 263 Broome Street,   "
ARNOLD, CONSTABLE & CO.,..............................307 Canal Street,   "
WM. H. WARNER, Esq.,...............................No. 3 Murray Street,   "
WM. A. BUTLER, Esq.,...Yonkers,   "
SYMONS & HAVENS,... ....Market, Brooklyn.
MIDDLETON & CO.,..... ....Shippers, Exchange Place, New York.
R. W. MILBANK, Esq.,.............................. No. 82 Front Street,   "
HENRY D. ROLPH, Esq.,...96 Bowery,   "
ALLAN C. WASHINGTON, Esq.,............................No. 30 Pine Street,   "
JAMES ROBINSON, Esq.,..............................No. 10 Burling Slip,   "
C. H. RAMSON, Esq.,..............................No. 11 West 25th Street,   "
CUMBERLAND MISSION SCHOOL,........(Dr. Cuyler's), Cumberland Street, Brooklyn.
LORIN PALMER, Esq.........Assist. Superintendent Plymouth Sabbath School,   "
JOSEPH LOCKITT & CO.,................... ....Pork Packers, Raymond Street,   "
D. & WM. H. MILLEMAN,.......... ... .   "   "   152 West Street, New York.
JOSEPH COLWELL, Esq.,.....................   "   "   230 West 27th St.,   "
H. M. & A. A. KIMBALL........ ....   "   "   126 Pond St., Providence, R.I.
FURMAN T. NUTT, Esq.,.....................................132 Fulton Street, New York.
LIVERPOOL & LONDON & GLOBE INS. COMPANY,......45 William Street,   "
JOHN SCHNEIDER, Esq.,.......................................Brewer, Brooklyn, E.D.
GILMAN, SONS & CO................................Bankers, 47 Exchange Place, New York.
GEORGE A. NICHOLS, Esq.,..548 Broadway, New York.
A. STOUT, Esq.................. ....Director Board of Freeholders, New Brunswick, N.J.
DR. HENRY FOSTER, ...Clifton Springs, New York.

WALTER KIMBALL, Esq.,...............................City Comptroller, Chicago, Illinois.
JOSEPH M. MOORE, Esq.,...........................Comptroller's Office, » »
VINCENT TILYOU, Esq.,.......................Pres't Arctic Insurance Co., New York.
A. S. HATCH, Esq.,......................................Banker (Fisk & Hatch), »
W. B. HATCH, Esq.,...........Firm of Fairbanks & Co., Scales, 253 Broadway, »
W. P. DOUGLAS, Esq.,...Yacht Sappho, »
MORGAN & SONS,.................................. Bankers, William Street, »
WM. PATON, Esq.,.................................. Importer, 345 Broadway, »
PRESBYTERIAN CHURCH, corner of Fifth Avenue & 19th Street, (Dr. Hall's), »
UNION CLUB ROOMS,....................Corner of 21st Street & 5th Avenue, »
PARKER HANDY, Esq.,..... Vice-Pres't Third National Bank, 29 Pine Street, »
NORTH ADAMS NATIONAL BANK,...............................North Adams, Mass.
JOHN L. FLAGG, Esq........ ....Troy, N. Y.
CHRISTIAN CHURCH,...........................28th Street, near Broadway, New York.
WM. E. DODGE, JR., Esq.,................Firm Phelps, Dodge & Co., Cliff Street, »
NEW BRUNSWICK COURT HOUSE,.....................New Brunswick, New Jersey.
EQUITABLE LIFE INSURANCE CO.,..New York.
H. B. HYDE, Esq.,................Vice-President Equitable Life Insurance Co., »
GEO. S. ALLAN,....................................... No. 20 Mansfield Place, »
H. K. BROWN,..Sculptor, Newburgh, »
MAGNUS GROSS.....Chairman of Com. on Hygienics, etc., Board of Education, New York.
WM. HITCHMAN, Esq...............................Clerk Board of Education, »
GEORGE S. NICHOLS, Esq......... ....548 Broadway, »
WM. W. SHERMAN, Esq....Firm of Duncan and Sherman, No. 9 Nassau Street, »
PROFESSOR CHARLES E. DAVIS................................ Poughkeepsie, »
D. L. NORTHRUP, Esq... .... Trustee School No. 19, Brooklyn, E. D.
J. S. BURR, Esq....Chairman Com. Warming and Ventilation. Brooklyn Board of Education.
HON. WM. B. ORTON....President West'n Union Tel. Company, 145 Broadway, New York.
JAS. D. REID, Esq.....................Editor Journal of Telegraph, 145 Broadway, »
J. C. HINCHMAN, Esq......Superintendent Metropolitan District Western Union Telegraph.
GRISWOLD GRAY, Esq., President Union Club, Corner of Fifth Ave. & 21st St., New York.
MELLEN & WILCOX.................................... ....158 Chatham Street, »
S. D. HATCH, Esq..................................Architect, 271 Broadway, »
JOHN BLOODGOOD & CO..........................Banker, 22 William Street, »
J. E. MILLER & CO............................Glenham Hotel, Fifth Avenue, »
WM. F. ALLEN, Esq.................................. ....Comptroller State of New York.
C. J. MARTIN, Esq....................President Home Insurance Co., Broadway, »
GERMAN SAVINGS BANK.........................100 East Fourteenth Street, »
P. BESSINGER, Esq.......................................President of German Savings Bank.
WM. VALENTINE, Esq........................... Principal School No. 19, Brooklyn, E. D.
CARTER & HAWLEY.... ....140 Pearl Street, New York.
SHOE & LEATHER BANK..271 Broadway, »
WM. ROBERTS...Architect, Newark.
GEO. PLATT.......................Architect, 329 Fourth Avenue, New York.
SHEPHERD KNAPP, Esq.........President of the Mechanics' Bank, Wall Street, »
HOME INSURANCE COMPANY...............................135 Broadway, »
GRINNELL, MENTURN & CO.. ... .78 South Street, »